"Mom, What is Peace?"

by Karl Ries

To Elisa
with best wishes!
Karl Ries

First Printing July 1997

ISBN 0-9659514-0-5

Published by

Karl Ries
3033 Ridge Top Road
Tyler, Texas 75703
(903) 839-3685

Acknowledgments

I am deeply indebted to Mrs. Hazel Edwards, Mrs. Joanne Jones and Mrs. Betty Nelson for their time and consideration in reviewing the manuscript and offering constructive criticism and helpful suggestions that have added considerably to this book. Especially, their tipoffs to some of the various German phraseologies, and their patient help with fittingly "Americanizing" these phrases. They deserve my warmest gratitude.

I am also truly thankful to my wife, Gisela, for her infinite patience and her never ending encouragements, during my work on certain chapters that often awakened depressing and painful memories.

Introduction

I have read, reread and reread the manuscript, in an attempt to select a particular chapter and topic which I believed might touch all readers and inspire them to read this narrative. However, as I believe all readers will find breathtaking, there is no single segment which stands out from the others. I find this fact to be a key in the overall value of this book. Therefore, I think it best to sum up my introduction as follows: There comes a time in each person's life, when we compare the shining moments of today with the sometimes shadowed events of the past in order to plan for the future.

In search for the answers, reasons and meanings of life, we are habitually guided by just one side of the story. Rarely do we see unbiased images of truths, such as those described in "Mom, What Is Peace?" This poignant topic provides an open window through which you see many visions of the past, present and future. "Mom, What Is Peace?" is not cluttered with historical data but outlines a tragic event from our past and some of the effects it had upon the growth of a child, the individual's development and lasting life effects. As you remain entrenched in these lines, you will continually ask yourself questions such as... *"Mom, What Is Peace?"*

— Gary Garrett, Ph.D.

Prologue

As a young child in Germany, I lived through World War II and its aftermath. This book tells of my varied childhood experiences. Imagine how terrible of an ordeal it must have been for the German civilian population and for the small child who wrote about it decades later. I strove to portray my impressions in an honest, informal, upbeat and positive way, with no desire to bore my readers with negative characterizations or whining self-pity.

Most Americans view Germany of that time as the villain not the victim. The unique element of this book is that it starts out in the style of a little nine year old boy. As the boy grows older and matures, the élan of telling his story matures right along with him.

Some friends felt that, because of the war, I must have been deprived of a "happy childhood," but this is not so. I perceive that term as relative. I certainly thought of myself as a happy child. A youngster growing up amongst war, bombs, sufferings and death can not possibly comprehend times of normality, peace and plenty, and is therefore unable to draw comparisons. I believe a child's capability to feel happy and make the best of things rests as much on the circumstances of his surroundings as on the individual personality of the child. Unfortunately, this often changes as the child "matures." It is also lamentable that such a hostile environment tends to harden a child's perception of the suffering of others and even of the value of a human life. This book was not intended to be a historical reference, but rather a narrative of my personal experiences.

The stated opinions, observations and emotions of the different characters are related just as they were encountered firsthand at that time and location.

— Karl Ries

Table of Contents

Chapter One

Empty Seats

With great pride and deep satisfaction I beheld the skyline of my beloved city. Rooftops, steeples, spires and chimneys paraded all around as I scanned the horizon from our roof-garden suite on top of an elegant apartment house. Munich, my cherished childhood home. We lived on the circular avenue around the grounds of the world-renowned Oktoberfest, the Bavaria Ring. The western horizon was dominated by the gigantic statue of the Bavaria. Especially after dark, during Oktoberfest time, the multitudes of lights were an unforgettable sight.

One golden sphere on top of a nearby building held a special meaning. When company came to visit, it was always one of my little pleasures to let them look out of our living room window and show them that golden sphere.

"That is where I will be going to school when I'm old enough," I would proudly explain, "it's right around the corner, so I'll never have far to walk." Everybody then envied me for my good fortune.

But alas, it all turned out so differently. By the fall of 1941, when I started school, this building had long been converted from an elementary school to a military hospital. My father had been drafted into service at the first day of the war. From then on, it was left to my mother and the employees to take charge of the store. My parents owned an automotive parts and accessory store a few blocks away and both had worked there full time. Because of that, it has always been only for short intervals in the early evenings and on Sundays that I would get to see them. And now, father was gone. The school I ended up having to go to was four miles away in a different part of the city. It was a long walk twice a day. Many other schools had met the same fate which caused severe overcrowding in the remaining ones. An entire day's curriculum had to be squeezed into a two hour session.

Our teacher, an elderly lady, was friendly and good natured, but she could also be different. In order to accomplish such a condensed program, there was no time for nonsense. There had to be strict discipline and she knew how to achieve that. We were seventy five boys in her class and some tended to be somewhat disorderly at first. When these distractions got too much for her, however, she smacked the stick she carried across one of the bench tops and hollered, "Silence!"

The resulting sudden stillness seemed almost spooky. We had quickly learned that she was ever willing to wrap that stick across our knuckles for even minor infractions. Many times she called a perpetrator to the front, made him hold out his hand and administered one or more hefty licks with her stick across his palm. Of course, everyone dreaded these trips to the front, but we soon respected her and we learned our stuff. There was, of course, plenty of homework every day but with only two hours of school plus two hours walking, we had plenty of time left to do it.

By the spring of 1942, the bomb raids on Munich, which had started as early as June of 1940, had increased considerably. Air raid sirens were wailing almost every night by then. Mostly incendiary bombs were used at that time. The horrible, high explosive TNT bombs came later. The damage done by these fire bombs, however, was serious enough. First, the roofs and attics of the houses burned off completely. All the while, the phosphorous liquid spilled downward, fiercely burning everything in its way. What was left were four- or five-storied gutted, empty ruins that kept on smoldering for days. Countless people perished in the flames as they were burnt alive. Many more became homeless and had to move in with friends or relatives that had, so far, been spared.

One morning in school, I found the seat beside mine vacant. Normally, my best friend, Freddy Rupp, would sit next to me. We had become buddies during the very early days of first grade and had been practically inseparable ever since. Like myself, he was an only child. He was of average build for his age and had light-blond hair. What had drawn me to him right from the start was his bubbly personality and the mischievous look in his big blue eyes. He was forever ready wherever there was any fun to be had, or to play little innocent tricks on anyone.

Freddy (in front) with class mates on
their walk home from school — 1941.

13

One day I was allowed to invite him to our home, so we could play together. That, however, was the one and only time. My mother felt that Freddy was too rambunctious. "I'd rather you wouldn't associate with the likes of him." she scolded. "He's much too wild. So don't bring him home anymore. Who knows what might get broken with him around here." Her blue eyes were blazing and I got the message. From then on, we played our games in the courtyard, on the streets, or in a nearby park.

Mother, in her mid-thirties at the time, was a rather stern woman and not to be disobeyed. Back-talk was just out of the question. Mother would have never tolerated it. But that's how she was. She was the youngest of three children, had constantly been spoiled by her parents and was utterly accustomed to always getting her way. It was not that she didn't love me or that she neglected me, she acted rather over-protective where I was concerned. Quite often this caused me to feel truly stifled. I had never been the type to quietly sit on the sofa and look pretty. From early on I had rebelled in my small ways against that sort of treatment. Open defiance was, of course, unthinkable but I would never concede to be conformed into some sofa doll. I was a boy, and that was that.

Upon asking our teacher where my buddy was, she told me that he and his family had been killed in the previous night's raid. This raid had been one of the more severe bombings of Munich so far. I was stunned. No more impish smile! I found it hard to envision his sparkling blue eyes forever closed and his lively body, or whatever was left of it, still and resting in some dark coffin.

14

Freddy, at one of our many "play grounds," two days
before he was killed in a bomb raid — 1942.

I felt hot tears coming, but couldn't afford to let
the rest of the class see that I was crying. I excused
myself, ran to the bathroom, and got sick. I had lost
my first true friend.

*

It wasn't long before his seat was occupied by some
other boy whose school had been destroyed by bombs.
This went on constantly and the turnover in students
was extraordinary. However, the sight of these empty
seats kept haunting me for many years to come.

The next evening, I found what I had been searching for in a long list of the local newspaper. Among the
hundreds of names of the bomb victims of two night
ago it said, "Alfred Rupp with wife and son". I remembered what Freddy had told me on our last visit to the
park. He had mentioned that his father was at home

15

on a brief leave from the West front. Now I saw the bitter irony: As a soldier, he had survived the war so far, only to be killed along with his entire family by a bomb at home on leave. I went to bed and cried myself to sleep.

*

During January of 1943, southern Germany experienced a fierce cold spell. Deep snow and thick ice covered everything. Folks, nevertheless, kept their sidewalks shoveled down to the last, hard layer of packed snow and ice. Walking had become a treacherous endeavor. Children, however, were expected to attend school regardless of the weather, and they did. Wrapped in heavy clothing and even in blankets, we endured the cold, made the best of it and still had fun playing games on our long track home. With all that extra clothing around you, you usually didn't get hurt when you took a spill on the ice. But, unfortunately, there was an exception:

School had let out at 10:30 a.m. and, on our way home, some of us decided to play "Choo Choo Train." We formed a line, hanging onto each others backpack. There were three of my classmates ahead of me and I was the caboose. Noisily, we chugged along the sidewalk, imitating all the racket of a real train. When the sidewalk ended, the lad up front stepped down onto the icy pavement. Suddenly, and without warning, the boys started running. I had paid no attention, was caught unawares and failed to let go of the backpack in front of me. I was dragged until I fell forward onto the sidewalk. My head hit the sharp edge of the curb with tremendous force. For a moment, I laid there stunned and with the wind knocked out of me. Then I quickly got up, not knowing how bad I was hurt. I felt warm blood gushing from my forehead which instantly covered my right eye. To my horror, I saw blood running down my coat, hopelessly soiling it.

I looked for my classmates but they had all disappeared. Feeling a slight dizziness, I stepped aside into the deep, unspoiled snow so I wouldn't slip again on the ice-glazed sidewalk. Again I looked down to examine my coat. It was a mess. I wondered what I would have to hear when I got home. Clothing was hard to replace in those days. Still looking down, I saw blood dripping onto the ground, creating little pink spots in the clean snow. I stood there, wondering what to do. My right eye was caked with blood and it seemed like I was looking through a crimson veil. I felt ashamed to be seen with such a terribly soiled coat. Freddy would have never deserted me like that, but alas, he was gone and I was alone.

Across the street I spied a tall stone wall. I headed for that and hid behind it. My head was still bleeding, but it didn't matter anymore; my coat was ruined. I just stood there, still not knowing what to do next. Being brought up during the stresses of war and by an often uncompromising mother can at times somewhat confuse ones priorities. Perhaps the bump on my head had something to do with it as well. Standing there, I don't know how long, I finally realized that I could not stay there forever. Regardless what people might think or say, I decided to go on home.

I had walked less than a minute, when a young lady came around a corner and saw me.

"Oh my God," she cried, "what happened to you, lad?" Her expression told of shock and concern.

"I fell and hit my head," I told her.

"Does it hurt badly? and where do you live?" she wanted to know.

"It doesn't really bother me," I replied truthfully and gave her my address.

"That's too far to walk," she told me, "take the tram and get home as fast as you can."

"Not the tram, Mother won't allow it," I explained.

She gave me a long, searching look, then she dug in her coat pocket, came up with a coin and gave it to me. She probably figured I didn't have any money. I handed it back to her, told her that I had money of my own, but that I could not go against Mother's well-meant order. It took her a moment to accept my position, then she took my hand and started walking.

"Where are we going?" I wanted to know.

"Well, since you wont ride the tram," she said with a reassuring smile, "I'm walking you home."

"But that's out of your way. I don't want to trouble you," I protested. When she had first showed up she had come from the opposite direction.

"No problem at all," she assured me, "Keep walking."

She told me her name was Erika. She looked to be about eighteen or nineteen and she was rather pretty. Most important, she was easy to talk to. To divert me from my misery, I supposed, Erika kept up an interesting conversation. People, when they saw us, gave us weird looks but nobody said anything. For that I was thankful. An hour flew by fast and before we knew it, we had arrived at our house. Erika rang the doorbell and when the buzzer sounded, we climbed upstairs.

The bleeding had stopped, so I didn't have to worry to get blood stains on the expensive carpeting of the elegant staircase. When we rounded the last turn, I saw Erna, our maid, up there, waiting at the landing. As she saw me, a look of horror appeared on her face.

"Oh my God, what happened to you?"

The same words that Erika had used when we first met. When I heard this, I started crying loudly and could not stop. I half heard Erika tell Erna where and how she found me. Erna thanked her and invited her inside, but Erika refused. Then Erna whisked me inside. Because of all my silly bawling, I didn't have a chance to thank Erika personally. This kept bothering me for a long time, but there was nothing I could do about it.

Erna called Mother at the store and she was there within five minutes. She was also shocked when she saw me. She immediately drove me to the Children's Clinic. She never did mention my soiled coat. When we arrived at the clinic, I was still crying. I didn't know why. I guess that it was just a delayed reaction, but I couldn't stop. The head wound took four stitches to close and I came away with my head prominently wrapped up. When my classmates saw me the next morning, everybody seemed to envy me for my formidable bandage. Thus, I became quite proud of it.

When the stitches were removed a week or so later, something went wrong. As the last stitch came out, the whole wound busted open again. The doctor told Mother that it could not be stitched a second time, and that a visible scar would remain. Mother was beside herself and refused to accept this, she made quite a

19

fuss. Later, our family doctor consoled her, saying that since I was a boy, a little scar like that wouldn't really matter. It didn't bother *me* at all.

*

As the war dragged on, heavier bombers started arriving over German cities, carrying more and more TNT bombs. A four-story house that received a direct hit by one of these collapsed completely, instantly becoming a useless pile of rubble. Schools and hospitals seemed to be prime targets, especially later when low-flying aircraft flew daytime raids and dropped their new, devastating, highly explosive TNT bombs. These soon became known as "Blockbusters". In the autumn of 1943, first our house and then my parent's business were destroyed. All the contents were demolished as well, including our piano on which I had just started taking lessons. Luckily, Mother and I had spent that night in our little weekend house in Starnberg or I would not be here to talk about it. Starnberg, at that time, was a small but popular summer resort about twenty miles south of Munich, at the shore of a beautiful lake amongst the foot hills of the Alps. From then on we lived there permanently but even there the school was severely overcrowded as more and more families from the city were evacuated to smaller towns and villages.

Allied Intelligence was well aware that Starnberg had no industry and no tight clusters of houses, and that there were no military targets. Because of this, Starnberg pretty well escaped the raids. However, even there were some exceptions: On September 6, 1943, a large hotel with public swimming pool facilities was attacked and destroyed by phosphor bombs. On June

13, 1944, dive bombers attacked and destroyed the firehouse and the municipal gym. Nine fire fighters were killed by fragment bombs and by direct hits from on-board cannons. The size of these buildings probably made them suspect of being schools or hospitals.

Chapter Two

"Mom, What is Peace?"

As early as 1940, only one year after the start of the great war, the streetcars and city buses in Munich as well as in other German cities had begun to run on reduced schedules. It was partly to save energy and partly because of shortages of maintenance parts and personnel. Just about all able-bodied men, including engineers and conductors, had been drafted into military service. The result was large crowds of people waiting at every tram and bus-stop. When a tram finally did appear, it was already overcrowded. People were standing on the running boards, hanging on to whatever protrusion they could find. Only grudgingly, room was made for those wanting to get off. Everyone was ready to quickly jump back on before the new crowd that had been waiting at the stop would have a chance to take their place.

The remaining conductors, usually old men, were helpless. Most often, they couldn't squeeze themselves through the tightly packed crowds of passengers to collect the fares. Many people got a free ride that way, but there was always a lot of arguing going on as everyone tried to look out only for themselves. It was not wise for children traveling alone to use trams or buses since they could easily be stepped on or even trampled by an indifferent crowd. That was why, when I entered school in the fall of 1941, I had been under strict orders from Mother never to ride the tram.

To conserve energy, the electrical power for the entire city population was shut off every weekday afternoon from two to six o'clock, which meant that during the winter months people had to spend some time in darkness or, if they were lucky to still have candles, by candlelight. This didn't bother me very much, as a matter of fact, I actually enjoyed these quiet late afternoons. I had to make sure that I was done with my homework before it got too dark to see, but usually that was no problem. What I really enjoyed were the days when Grandpa was visiting. He would sit with us in the gathering dusk and tell stories. I remember asking him for spooky stories or mysteries, which I loved best. I became so engrossed listening to him, that it was often actually a disappointment for me when, at six p.m., the lights came back on.

Due to shortages of material of every kind, the quality of products, sold to the public, suffered dearly. Shoes were made of cheap cloth with wooden soles, clothing contained recycled paper, hardware items were of the same inferior quality, nails were so soft that they would bend, building materials contained straw, and so on. Gone was the world-renowned German quality. In spite of all this, production never kept up with demands and the resulting shortages became an everyday occurrence. Besides shortages there were a lot of items that were totally unavailable. But soon there were substitutes for just about everything. Instead of coffee from imported coffee beans we drank a brown broth made of malt or roasted barley. It was called "Ersatz Kaffee" (coffee substitute.) There was an Ersatz for a lot of things and one either made do with Ersatz or go without. Rock candy, the brown kind, the one with the string in it, was used for sweeteners instead of sugar. The clear kind was eaten as candy. There was even a substitute for chocolate but it tasted awful and had a very unpleasing, mealy texture. It was the only chocolate children knew, so we ate it. The stories that people dreamily told of exquisite pralines, candy and other delights didn't mean much to children who had never had the pleasure of tasting them or had been too young to remember them now.

The part that I noticed the most was the poor quality of the few still available toys. The toys still produced were, to the greatest extent, war-toys. There were little soldiers in all the different colors of the German military in various body positions, and holding assorted weapons. There were tanks, canons, military vehicles and air planes. While these were at least made of cheap metal, the soldiers were made of a brown substance that looked like dried mud (the children called it something else.) They frequently broke when dropped but what was worse, they didn't even survive realistic play. We used to set them up outdoors in battle formations about ten feet apart and then threw marbles or pebbles at each other's installations. We would have been quite happy to count the soldiers that fell over as battle losses. But they didn't just fall over, they crumbled with nearly every hit. Even the marbles were made of the same brown substance and we had to take care not to step on one. As the war progressed, ready-made toys were gradually being replaced by cheap do-it-yourself kits that had to be glued together from pre-printed paper and cardboard. While children had fun in building these, they never really lasted very long.

Gone were the days when you could buy the famous little Schuco cars or the Märklin trains or erector sets. Only few children still had some of these priceless possessions that had been handed down to them from an older sibling. These had become valuable trade items. If you had some useful item to trade, or a fifty-penny coin that you were willing to spend, you could trade, not for these toys themselves, but for the privilege of playing with them for an hour or so. I had no siblings, therefor I had very few pre-war toys.

Untold other inconveniences also bothered me. But all in all, I had soon found that there was no use in complaining about overcrowded trams, long lines, poor quality, or uninteresting toys. I found little sympathy. No matter who I talked to, the answer invariably was, "It's the War! Ah, but in peacetime..."

Whenever a shipment of goods arrived at a store, people stood in long, slow-moving lines to buy whatever it was that had come in that day. Virtually everything was rationed. Food items, when available, were distributed only against monthly ration cards. For clothing, shoes, and certain hardware items, a procurement slip was needed. To obtain one of these required a "Document of Urgency" and even these were graded, according to the degree of urgency. It was a hassle all around to obtain even the most necessary item needed for everyday living. Things that used to be imported quickly vanished completely from the lists of availability. There were, for instance, no more bananas, oranges or any other tropical fruits and their important vitamins and minerals were sorely missed. What little citrus fruit was still available by imports from Italy was strictly reserved for the military. Later, as the tide of war started turning against Germany, Italy promptly switched her loyalty to the enemy Allies. Now, even that source of fruit had dried up.

"Mom," I remember asking when I was six years old, "why is everything so complicated and why are there always these long lines of people everywhere?"

"It's because of the war," she said, "In peacetime it all was different."

She probably thought me too young to understand and just left it at that.

The situation for the German civilian population gradually worsened. People found themselves under more and more pressure. The constant threat from nightly bombings plus the brutal change of lifestyle that the war forced on people gradually transformed their behavior for the worse. I was by now eight years old and, of course, I was not aware of these reasons. All I noticed were the changes. Formerly benevolent, calm and helpful individuals had suddenly become unfriendly, selfish, jealous, pushy and, some of them, downright nasty.

I remember asking Mother one day why the people act that bad. She looked at me and, sadly shaking her head, said, "The people are not really bad, they're just under pressure from all the shortages and inconveniences caused by the war."

"Mom, that's not true," I blurted, interrupting her well-meant explanations, "People are bad. I saw it myself only last week at Dreher's bakery where you sent me for bread. I stood there since six o'clock in the morning and even though they only opened at nine, there were a lot of people waiting ahead of me already. We were standing on the many steps that lead up to the door, when a few places ahead of me, a little girl fainted, fell and rolled down most of the steps. There she laid and no one would look after her. When she came to a few minutes later, her money and her ration stamps, that had dropped from her hands, and even her satchel were gone. Although she was so weak that

27

she could hardly stand, she was sent to the very end of the line. No one would allow her to go back to her rightful place. Shortly after I got our bread, they were sold out and that little girl could not get anything, even if she would still have had her money and her stamps."

"Who was that girl?" Mother wanted to know.

"I don't know," I said. "I think she belongs to one of those refugee families that had come from the East, running away from the Russians. I wanted so much to go and help her but I would have lost my place as well. But it really doesn't matter who she was, this happens a lot to children. It happened to me too. I just never told you about it because I didn't want to worry you. Last month, as I was standing in line at the dairy store, an old man who stood behind me suddenly said to me, 'Little boy, you should let an old man like me get in front of you.' With that he grabbed me and pushed me behind himself. I wouldn't have minded that too much, but now the person behind me complained that I didn't belong there and started pushing me to the rear as well.

"I know you taught me to act respectful and be polite to older people, but that was just too much. I protested loudly and as that didn't help I started screaming. I got attention. From somewhere in the line behind me, old Mr. Kergl, who knew me, began arguing with the old man that had started it all. While no one left their place in the line, they were hollering back and forth at each other. Other people started shouting too, some even in my favor. While everyone's attention was focused on these two old men, I slipped back to my original place and tried to act as unobtru sive as possible."

"You did the right thing, son," Mother said after thinking awhile, "While it is very important that you respect your elders and that you are polite to people, it doesn't mean you have to hold still to injustices and bullying behavior. I know there is sometimes just a very fine line between being right and being belligerent, but you were perfectly justified in how you acted.

"But as I was trying to explain to you before," she patiently rationalized, "the people aren't really bad, it's just that some of them react violently to the unusual pressures and stresses that are caused by the war, while most others, like your Mr. Kergl, are still trying to act civilized. Back during peacetime, people didn't act that way at all," she explained.

*

"Mom, you keep talking so much about peacetime," I cornered her one day, "Mom, what is *peace?*"

"It was simply the time before this war broke out," she replied evasively.

"But I want you to tell me all about this," I insisted, "I just don't understand the meaning of peace. I want to know all about it, and why it isn't anymore as it used to be."

Mother had been folding her laundry at the time. She looked at me and probably realized that I would not be put off this time, and that I needed some answers. She sat down on the sofa and told me to sit with her.

"Peace was the time between the two wars," she began. "Then, life was normal. Money still had real value and everything one could wish for was available as long as one had the money to pay for it. Now we still need money, but without ration cards or procurement slips money is of little use."

"You mean that you could walk into a store and buy as many chocolate bars as you liked?" I asked.

"Yes, my boy," she chuckled, "they practically threw it at you. They were happy that you bought it from them, instead from one of their competitors."

"Tell me more," I begged. What I had heard was so overwhelming that I just couldn't let it hang there.

"Well," she said after awhile, "it was the same with imports. Imports are goods one country buys from another country mainly because these goods are not available locally. Oranges and bananas, for instance do not grow in our harsh climate. So our merchants bought them from foreign lands all over the world. These countries were just too happy to sell them to us. As soon as the war started, however, it didn't take long and there were no more imports."

I thought about all this but found it hard to imagine how different it must have been during those legendary peacetimes.

"Why do there have to be wars?" I asked, "Why can't it remain peacetime always?"

"Son, there are many reasons for war," she replied, "There can be disputes between countries just as between people and neighbors. These disputes can sometimes escalate into war. Then, throughout history, there are always certain people that profiteer from wars. They are always ready to instigate or step up trouble wherever they see the opportunity for a new war to break out. They themselves, however, stay hidden in the background and profit from other people's misery.

They are the ones that will do everything in their power to keep old hates alive," she explained.

"How can anyone profit from war, all I see so far is misery?" I asked.

"A lot of these people own or control the factories that produce war materials such as tanks, guns, ammunition, fighter-aircraft bombers and bombs. Without war there would be little demand for these things. They would be forced to produce normal consumer goods for which there might be only a limited demand, especially with heavy competition from other producers."

After Mom finished explaining to me the meaning of consumer goods, she continued,

"However, as long as there are wars, they don't have to worry about being able to sell their wares, and usually at outrageously inflated prices. It all will be paid for by the involved governments with tax money extracted from its citizens. There will be an insatiable demand as long as there is a war somewhere.

"Also, wars are often incited by outsiders between nations that these outsiders perceive as a threat to themselves. They correctly count on it that one or all of these warring nations will be severely weakened and thus no longer present a threat to themselves."

Here my mind flashed back to the incident on the steps of the bakery where the two old men were fiercely arguing and where I had been quite happy to see the attention drawn away from me. This had given me the opportunity to quickly reclaim my rightful place in the line. I thought about the similarities but I didn't say anything.

"I'm sure," Mother continued, "there may be many other reasons for war, but these seem to be the most obvious ones."

"But who decides if a country should go to war, Mom?" I asked.

"Usually the government of a country," she replied.

"Now what started this war?" I wanted to know.

"Germany was finally trying to set right the injustices forced on her by the enemy as the result of our losing the first World War. A lot of land had been taken from us and given to other countries. Then Germany was forced to pay really unreasonably high reparation costs for that war. This slowly but surely bled our economy to the point of no return. Runaway inflation and stupendous unemployment followed. Then one day, our military started to take back some of our land and moved into the areas of Germany that had been taken from us after the last war."

"If Germany was as poor as you say," I interrupted, "where did the money come from to build up such a strong military?"

"That, my son, is a good question." she mused, "There certainly had to have been help from somewhere outside.

"But as I was saying," she continued, "we were taking back the land from Poland, Czechoslovakia and from France that had been rightfully ours all along. But then, and this I could never understand, all of a sudden, it no longer seemed enough. Our expansion quickly continued into western Russia. England, so far entirely unconcerned, unexpectedly felt it would have to try and come to the aid of Poland. It also claimed it felt threatened itself and declared war on Germany. Then, through the interference of other uninvolved third parties, a purely local conflict finally escalated into the full-fledged World War that we are experiencing now."

"Who do you think will win this war, Mom?" I asked.

"Who can say, I hope we will," she added. "You know that I have little regard for our Nazi dictatorship, but if we lose this war as well then I don't foresee any future for Germany or for you and me. Our enemies will really destroy us this time if they can. All we can do is pray for a fast victory."

Chapter Three

An Unexpected Windfall

To give regular pocket money allowances to children was not a common practice in those days. However, by sheer coincidence, I had found a way to come up with plenty of fifty-penny coins to rent other children's playthings.

One day in school, we were informed that a government agency was offering a bounty on poisonous snakes. The only such snake in Germany is the Kreuzotter, an adder with cross-like markings along its back. I knew where they could be found but I knew nothing about how to catch and kill them.

My grandparents on my mother's side still lived in Munich and the very next time Grandpa came to visit, I asked him about catching snakes. He was eagerly willing to help. From a beech-wood branch he whittled a forked stick. The points of the fork were sharpened and the whole thing was about three feet long. He told me to pin the snake to the ground between the two points of the stick and close behind the snake's head. Then I was to cut off its head and pop it into a paper sack. The janitor at our school, collecting these heads for that agency, promptly paid fifty pennies apiece for them.

The next day after school, equipped with my stick, a sharp knife and a paper sack I hiked to a spot in a nearby forest that I knew harbored a fair number of these snakes. In a small clearing there were some large flat rocks scattered on the ground. The snakes were known to lay on these rocks to sun themselves. It was a warm and pleasant day. Only occasionally, small clouds drifted before the sun. I watched the shadows of these clouds, now on the rocks, and now on the grass. A slight breeze made the leaves quiver and dance and their shadows played and died as another cloud sailed overhead.

Just as I had expected, several snakes were present when I arrived there. All of them, however, were on the rocks. In order to pin them I had to first get them onto soft ground. I picked the closest one and scraped it off the rock with my stick. As it tried to slither away I used the forked end of the stick to pin its body to the ground, close behind its head. I leaned on the other end of the stick to hold it there. It had been a perfect aim. As I reached for my knife, however, the snake's body started whipping back and forth so fiercely that it managed to pull its head out from under the fork. I was just barely able to knock its head aside as it started striking at me. When I jumped back, it quickly disappeared into the high grass that surrounded the rocks. I wasn't sure what had caused this mishap. Either I hadn't pushed down hard enough on the stick or one of the points had encountered rock, in any case, by whipping its body it had been able to free itself. I realized how lucky I had been not to get bitten. I had enough for that day. I knew I somehow had to improve on this method of catching snakes.

That night it occurred to me that if I had a second forked stick, I could pin its body a second time a little farther back. This should keep the whipping in check and away from its head. The following day I whittled another fork and tried it again. I came up on a snake in the grass near the rocks. It was not yet moving and I had no trouble placing my first stick where I wanted it. Bearing down on this with one hand, I placed the fork of the second stick behind the first, drew about a foot down the snake's body and pinned it once again. As much as the tail end whipped, there was no further strain on the front stick that held down the head. Placing both sticks in one hand and bearing down, I reached for my knife with my free hand and cut off it's head with no further problems. I picked it up with the point of my knife and placed it into the paper sack. Grandpa had warned me not to put my hands into that bag for a good while. He said I could still get hurt. I was mindful of his well-meant advice and caught two more snakes that afternoon. The next day, I collected three fifty-penny coins at school. Now I had money to rent other children's toys. Occasionally, I brought a few more snake heads to school, but my unexpected windfall was yet to come.

In school one morning, just before classes started, I got caught drawing funny pictures of our teacher onto the large blackboard. I meant to cover my masterpiece by folding the other blackboard over it, so it wouldn't be discovered until well into the class. But alas, the teacher showed up too soon and didn't appreciate my talents at all. To the amusement of my classmates, I was sent for solitary confinement. The janitor was summoned and he escorted me down to the basement. Since they wouldn't let me out for recess, I was allowed to take my sandwich with me. After he had locked me in, I at first stood in complete darkness. It didn't take long, however, and my eyes became adjusted to the absence of light. I started to make out details about the large room and its content. Not that there was much to look at. First, I noticed an old, damaged school bench. I promptly sat down on it and felt a lot more comfortable. Then I discovered that what little light entered the room, came from the cracks around the doors that covered the coal chute.

I was soon bored and wanted to explore my surroundings more thoroughly. For this I needed light. I felt my way to the coal doors. They were secured with a padlock from the outside. However, by prying up on them I was able to wedge a piece of coal into the crack to hold it open as much as the lock allowed. Climbing up onto the pile of coals and peeking through, I saw that the doors led to the school yard. The enlarged crack now allowed sufficient light into the dark basement for me to see by. Mainly, what I saw were uninteresting supplies, the furnace, a table with a lot of shadowy cans and bottles on it, some other implements and a lot of junk, and then, there was the box.

It was a large cardboard box which had been placed on some pieces of leftover lumber. In looking into the box I became aware of some undefinable things that rolled along its bottom as I was tilting the box. At first, I thought of small pine cones but I soon decided that whatever it was looked smaller than that. I then dragged the entire box over to the coal bin and by the light from above I was able to recognize its grisly contents. Momentarily, I was startled. The box contained all the snake heads that had been collected so far. Apparently the agency that was responsible to pick them up from the school had not yet bothered to do so. With all the turmoil caused by the war I figured the whole thing had probably become very unimportant. Thinking about it, I found it highly unlikely that they would ever be collected.

It was then that the idea first materialized. I returned the box to where I had found it and searched the rest of the basement without, however, finding anything else of interest. The thought about what I was planning to do with those heads was exciting and left little room for anything else. I forced myself to calm down, sat on the bench and started eating my lunch. I knew that it was too early, the recess bell hadn't sounded yet, but I needed the paper sack that contained my sandwich.

When I had finished eating, I again moved the large box to where there was more light. Using an old coal shovel I carefully scooped enough heads into my lunch bag to fill it. After recess was over and no one would be likely to enter the school yard, I pried up on the wings of the door and slid the bag out into the open. I hoped it wouldn't be too visible in case someone would enter the yard, but that was a chance I just had to take. I removed the coal from the crack and put everything back in order. Then I set myself comfortably onto that bench and promptly fell asleep. Shortly before school was over the janitor came and delivered me to our teacher. After listening to a little sermon about how distracting and disrespectful my actions had been, I was allowed to go home. Immediately, I snuck into the school yard to look for my bag. Nobody had found it and I quickly stashed it inside my luggage.

The very next day, I delivered five heads to the janitor who promptly handed me five coins. Now I brought in heads quite regularly, never having any problems in collecting my bounty. Only once did he remark about the heads looking kind of dry and shriveled, but I told him that I had had them for awhile, which really was no lie. The man was satisfied and paid the bounty. From then on I always had enough coins to rent any toy for as long as it held my interest. I knew that should I ever need more, all I had to do was to earn myself another spell in that dark basement.

Chapter Four

Buried Alive

I was nine years old and I was enjoying the 1944 summer vacation. One morning, my mother told me that we would go to Stuttgart and stay with her cousin for a few days. I remembered Aunt Anne and Uncle Richard. They had visited with us several times in past years. The last time, Aunt Anne had showed up alone. Uncle Richard had been drafted and was fighting on the western front. They had no children of their own and seemed to enjoy playing with me, while I relished the extraordinary attention.

I looked forward to this trip as a welcome diversion before school started again. Stuttgart, while smaller than Munich, was a beautiful city. The main part of it was located in a large valley, while the outer perimeter climbed up the surrounding hills on all sides. It was about one hundred and fifty miles from Munich, but the train ride was long and tedious. Stations and tracks had by now received countless bomb hits. Temporary repairs and reroutings turned this three hour trip into a seven hour drudgery.

Damage to the rail system caused long delays for civilian travel.

Aunt Anne lived on the second floor of a large apartment house in a residential section of the city. It was four stories tall and had five numbered entrances facing the street. Hers was number nine on the far end. Mother and I walked up the concrete stairway that led to her apartment. Both of us were glad to have that boring trip behind us. Aunt Anne was delighted to see us. She had been awaiting our arrival eagerly but without being overly worried about our long delay. Those things were by now common, everyday occurrences. She was about the same age and build as Mother but of a quite different, more easy-going temperament. She was rather pretty with her shoulder-length dark brown hair and her sparkling blue eyes with their often mischievous twinkle. However, her humor seemed honest and sincere, while Mother's usually was more of the teasing kind. At times, it had even seemed rather devious to me.

The three of us had a great time together. Then, after two days, Mother went on to another city where she had some business to take care of. She said she would pick me up again on her way home. Three days later, however, came word that, due to severe bomb-damage to the railway system, she was forced to take a different route home. Aunt Anne was supposed to put me on a train to Munich where Mother would be waiting for me.

My aunt, however, seeing how I liked it there, offered to have me stay on for a few more days. I was happy. I played with the neighborhood children, welcomed the change of scenery and especially the lack of chores. Aunt Anne would not let me help with anything. She told me to enjoy my vacation, and I did. It felt like heaven.

Then one night, she woke me from my sleep. I could hear the awesome, bone-chilling wail of the air-raid sirens. I had almost forgotten about them because since we had left Munich and lived in the little town of Starnberg, I had no longer heard the sirens. They had been going off at rare times in Starnberg as well, but Mother had never bothered to wake me.

There had been occasional bomb raids on Stuttgart so far, but not as severe and as numerous as on Munich and other German cities. My aunt helped me to get dressed and said we'd have to go to the bomb shelter. She had, like many people by now, become rather indifferent to the alerts and hadn't bothered to go to shelters anymore, but since she felt responsible for me she insisted that we go. I was too sleepy to protest and went along without a fuss.

The basement of the apartments on the other the end of the building was being used as a bomb shelter for all the residents of the complex who chose to use it. In utter darkness we walked down the sidewalk to the first entrance, where an old man with a dimmed flashlight ushered us down a flight of steps. There were about twenty five sleepy looking people sitting on benches and upturned buckets. The basement was no different than any other I had seen in other city houses except that the ceiling was shored up with many telephone poles. Boards were wedged in at the top of the timbers to keep those upright supports in place.

As the old man showed us to a bench at the far end, I felt like I was walking through a forest because of all those timbers. The room was dimly lit by one blue light bulb. I saw a couple of old men, women of every age and one little boy. He looked to be about three years old and I felt drawn to him right away as the only possible playmate to pass the time with. He was a rather lively fellow with blond hair and big innocent blue eyes that seemed to look straight into one's soul. He was of such a trusting nature that one had to like him instantly. His name was Hansi and as soon as my aunt and I were settled down on a bench at the far wall, Hansi came over and started talking. He had a little toy car in his hand and in no time we were playing happily together on the cold concrete floor, totally forgetting our dreary surroundings. Every once in a while he would toddle over to the other side to reassure himself that his Mommy was still there, but he always came running back to play "cars" with me.

Then, a young man, which I had not noticed so far and who had been sitting near the entrance, came over and talked to us kids and even played "cars" with us. He was the only young man present. He was a soldier, he told us, home on leave from the eastern front, and this was his last day before he had to join his comrades once again. However, he didn't stay long and returned to his place to chat with his mother, who had been sitting quietly next to the entrance.

We had been in that basement for about twenty minutes, when suddenly we heard what sounded like a string of distant explosions, followed shortly by another series, this time much louder and closer. Then came a deafening blast and with it a stunning shockwave. The light had gone out and in total darkness we heard a seemingly never ending rumble that got louder and louder. We knew instantly that the building had been hit and was collapsing on top of us. Then came the sound of cracking timbers and fearful screams as an avalanche of concrete, bricks and rubble filled the basement. Just as suddenly, it was still once again. There were a few weak whimpers and moans, but they faded quickly. The silence was eerie and only occasionally interrupted by some debris falling onto the floor. I heard some uncertain whispers, then someone turned on a flashlight. The dust hung in the room so thick you could not make out anything. Now I became aware of the dust and grit in my mouth and nose and eyes. I called out for my aunt. She had been already searching for me and kept screaming for whoever had that flashlight to help her find me. When she did find me, she grabbed my arm and hung on to it as if she was afraid that I could run away. I had no intention of running, besides, there was no place to run to.

From below us, we heard soft crying. It came from under our bench. I reached down and felt around for Hansi. The shock wave from the explosion had blown him under the bench and he was lying down there, whimpering. Then he started to cry for his Mommy. In the dark, I pulled him up and supported him in front of me. Then someone turned the flashlight back on. By its shine I could finally see Aunt Anne and Hansi. They both seemed unhurt, but oh how they looked! Their hair, their faces and their clothing were completely white from the dust and they looked like ghosts. The only thing that was distinguishable was their mouths where they had licked their lips and had spit out the grit. Later on I found out that the few other survivors, including myself, were covered with dust as well, and that we looked no different from them.

As most of the airborne debris had settled, we slowly began to comprehend the extent of the terrible tragedy. The entire far side of the basement had collapsed in spite of all the timbers, and nothing but a pile of rubble was visible. The exit had been on that side and was now totally buried. My mind at first refused to accept the bitter reality and I hoped I would soon wake up from this terrifying nightmare. But it all was only too real. The city houses were made of bricks, mortar and concrete, the weight of which was tremendous. We followed the flashlight's beam to our side and found that only a narrow space had held up and kept us from being crushed. The few remaining timbers were cracked and standing at crazy angles, but so far, they seemed to hold.

After the worst of the shock began to wear off, people counted heads and came up with a total of only seven persons. There was my aunt, Hansi, the old man and his wife, their name was Kolb, another old woman, a Mrs. Unger and her daughter, Mrs. Fischer. The fate of the rest of them could easily be guessed.

There were no more bomb explosions to be heard and soon we could faintly make out the steady tone of the "all clear" sirens. For Stuttgart it was over, at least for this time, but what about us? We had no way to get out of our small prison. Everybody hoped and prayed that our part of the shelter would at least hold up until we would be found and dug out.

My aunt still held me by my arm and I was hanging on to little Hansi. She would not let go until I promised to stay close. The worst thing for me was when Hansi kept asking where his Mommy was and when he wanted to go over there to find her. I guessed alright what had happened to her but I couldn't possibly tell the truth to this trusting and innocent little boy. When he couldn't go and no answer came to his calls, he again started crying. We did our best to calm him down. We bedded him down on our bench as well as we could.

His crying turned to fitful whimpering until he finally fell asleep. After awhile, when he awoke, it started all over again. During the times when Hansi was sleeping, I would, in spite of my promise, often wander about in the remaining space to stretch my aching limbs. Like everyone else, I had bruises and scrapes from flying debris but I didn't think I was badly hurt. Of course, I couldn't be sure.

On one such excursion, I had felt my way as far back to the rubble as I could. Then someone turned on the flashlight. Right in front of me, illuminated by the feeble light was a women's hand. Crusted blood covered her ring finger, but her golden wedding band plainly reflected in the weak light. Even though my stomach was empty I felt I would be sick. The light was switched off again and I groped my way back to my aunt in the dark. I told her what I had seen. She tried her best to calm me down, then she told Mr. Kolb about it. The old man got the flashlight and went back there. He started working with the rubble. His back was hiding from us what he was doing. Suddenly one piece of concrete shifted, starting others tumbling in a small slide. The old man, flinging himself aside, managed not to get hit. As the rumble subsided and the dust settled, the hand was no longer visible. I heard Mr. Kolb say that it had felt cold and lifeless and that whoever it was, was beyond help.

Only two people had a wrist watch, Mr. Kolb and Mrs. Unger. Hers, however was damaged and it no longer worked. According to Mr. Kolb, it was by now midmorning and everyone started complaining of thirst and hunger. In her handbag, Mrs. Kolb had brought a section of cake with her. This was now shared equally amongst the seven people. The thirst, however, was worse. As I was finished forcing down that dry cake, I would have given anything for a glass of water. On our way in earlier, I had noticed several large cisterns full of water and a massive wooden box filled with sand. These had been near the entrance door and were placed there to put out a possible fire. They were by now, however, under the rubble, out of reach and of no use to any of us.

Realizing that it had to be full daylight outside, it was time to let someone know that there were survivors under all that destruction. We needed to be dug out, hopefully in time before the rest of the shelter collapsed or before we starved to death. The usual method was to take a brick and knock it against the walls. Outside in broad daylight, someone always listened for such signals after each bomb raid and many people had so far been rescued from certain death. For us, however, it remained as dark as it had been since the building had collapsed. We were in absolute darkness. Now we all took turns with the brick. I even appreciated taking my turn at the knocking, since it gave me something to do to break the monotony and kept me from thinking. However, by evening of that day, no response could be heard.

At nightfall there was a debate amongst the adults whether we should keep the knock signals up during the whole night. Some felt that there would be no one out there to look for us in the dark of night. Others argued that at night, with the absence of street noise and traffic, our signals could be heard more clearly if someone happened to pass nearby. That argument finally won and from then on the noise of the knocking never ceased for the entire duration of our ordeal. It was always the same, seven knocks, then silence to listen for a response, then seven more knocks, and so on.

Whether it was out of nervousness or just to be sure not to forget it, every ten minutes, it seemed, Mr. Kolb was winding his watch. I remember thinking that if he would overwind it, it would break and we would have no idea at all what time it was. Thirst then started to really bother me and I complained to my aunt about it, knowing quite well that she really couldn't do a thing about it. But to my great surprise, she said that she knew how to ease my need. She told me to feel around on the concrete floor to try and find some small stones or pebbles. I did as I was told but wondered what that could have to do with my being so thirsty. When I brought her what I had found, she rejected all the little pieces of rubble and told me that we wanted smooth, round, clean pebbles without concrete or mortar on them. That was a tall order. After all, I thought, it wasn't a quarry that had entombed us, but a large house. So where should these clean pebbles come from? But I took up the search again, suspecting that she just did that to keep me occupied. I finally found some pieces that were a little smoother and told her that it was the best I could do. When the flashlight came on again, my aunt wiped the worst dust off them and gave two of them back to me.

"Put these in your mouth," she said, "It will ease your thirst. Just don't swallow them or chew on them."

I tried it, expecting some kind of taste from them, but I was disappointed.

"Yech," I said, "they taste like mud!"

"That's all right, they'll help you nevertheless." She

then took the rest of the pebbles and put them into her own mouth. I did not know how it worked, but somehow it did seem to help some. I had to go to the bathroom again. There was none, of course. One of the buckets had been used for that. Then it had been pushed into the furthest corner of our little enclosure. I had gone several times already since we were in that basement, but by this time the stench was overwhelming. Holding my nose with one hand, I did what I had to do and couldn't get away from that bucket fast enough. The stink, however, seemed to follow me and from then on I could smell it all the time.

Intermittently, people prayed but the noisy knocking never ceased. I was getting very restless by then. The smell, the noise, the darkness, everything started to get on my nerves and I guess I didn't make it any easier for my poor aunt. She promised me all kind of good things that she would do for me once we were rescued. Thinking of cookies and cake and perhaps even a visit to the zoo, I drifted off into a fitful sleep. It didn't sink in that there really couldn't be any cookies or cake, since everything was on rations.

Waking up, more thirsty than ever before, I took my pebbles from my pocket and put them back in my mouth. They, however, seemed to have lost their magic and proved less and less effective. My mouth was parched, my throat was parched and sore, and I was so hungry that my stomach cramped.

Another day had gone by, according to Mr. Kolb's watch. Hansi was by now more dead than alive. We took care of him as best as we could, but there was nothing we could do to relieve his thirst and his hunger or to bring his Mommy back. He was too weak to cry and, I guessed, too dried up for tears. He refused to go near that bucket and before we realized what he had done, he started smelling just as bad.

Then another odor started to drift in from the huge pile of debris. From the beginning, we had noticed a weak current of fresh air coming from somewhere through that collapsed part of the shelter. Not much, but enough to keep us alive. Since no large openings were visible, nobody dared to check it out to see where it might come from. We all knew only too well that the slightest shifting might bring on the total collapse of what was left of the shelter. But where welcome fresh air used to seep in, this awful stench seemed to gradually become stronger. It was different than the bucket, but nauseating just the same. Mr. Kolb thought it might be sewer gas from a broken pipe. Then I overheard the women whispering that it might be coming from the Dead under that rubble. This was the first time that I became scared.

I tormented my aunt to tell me about the Dead, the smell, and if the Dead could also come in here. She hushed me up and refused to talk about any dead people. My imagination, however, ran wild and from then on I stayed much closer to her than before. I dreaded to go anywhere near that other side, fearing what it may hold or what might come out from there.

Whenever it wasn't my turn with the brick, I spent most of my time curled up on the bench, sleeping. I was just too weak and worn to do anything else. I had by now gotten used to the noise, the stench and the darkness. What did not get any better was the thirst and hunger. Another night had gone by when I awoke to some considerable excitement. Aunt Anne told me that a response had been heard to our knock signals. I listened to the familiar knock rhythm, then a pause, and then I clearly heard a similar knocking from far away and from above. This perked up most of us except for little Hansi; he was out of it by now. He was not yet dead, but too weak to respond to any efforts to rouse him. The women prayed again, much louder this time and much more intensely. Knock signals were going back and forth, soon to be followed by noises of a different kind. It sounded like shovels digging and sometimes the occasional shouting, but from very far away. Mr. Kolb said it was 8:30 in the morning and told us to hang on.

"It won't take them much longer," he said, "now that they know we're in here."

At 12:30, the digging had become much louder and closer, and stones started raining down on some of us. We crowded into the corner farthest away from that area. Suddenly we could see a faint trace of daylight from somewhere high above. Right after that, a shovel appeared through a new opening in the ceiling. More dirt came down. The digging had stopped. Then someone called down to us. He wanted to know how many of us there were. My aunt, being closest, told him that there were seven of us and asked for water. Our rescuers must have been prepared for this, because almost instantly, a bottle full of water came sliding down the inclined tunnel. My aunt caught it, but that wasn't even necessary; it had been secured with a string. Most of us drank some, then it was hauled up and immediately refilled. Again and again the filled water bottle would come sliding down. Everybody drank greedily and then we realized how hungry we were. But that just had to wait.

When everyone had enough for awhile, we stepped back from the hole, so they could work on making it big enough to get us out. The dust was almost as bad as it had been when the building had collapsed, but we all welcomed the fresh air that had started to come in as well.

Finally, the digging stopped once again. Someone hollered down to us to start handing the children up. Mrs. Fischer, the tallest, picked up Hansi and carefully pushed his lifeless figure up the hole as far as she could reach. The poor little guy was not aware of what was happening to him, he only moaned a little and didn't move. Then we saw his feet disappear as someone pulled him all the way up. I was next. Aunt Anne and Mrs. Fischer lifted me and told me to stretch both arms up as far as I could and then they pushed me up.

A large calloused hand reached down to me. Closing around both of my wrists, it gingerly pulled me up and through a very tight opening into the blinding daylight. Although it was a grey and drizzly day, the unaccustomed light dazzled my eyes as if it were the brightest sunlight. When my eyes finally got adjusted to it, I could see that it was a tall old man that had pulled me up. Now he was sticking his head into the opening and asked for any other children. There were none. He told the people to get back as far as possible so he could try and enlarge the opening for them. Everyone inside as well as outside was fully aware that the rest of the basement could collapse at any moment. This would have meant the end for the people still inside. Through the hole I heard again intense praying as the man worked carefully to enlarge the opening. Several women helped move the debris that he cleared and handed back to them.

As I sat on a piece of concrete near the hole, a vehicle drove up. It had once been an old Mercedes 4-door passenger car but by now it served as a makeshift ambulance with large Red Cross symbols painted on its sides. I saw how some people handed Hansi to an attendant who placed him on the back seat. His little toy car fell out of his coat pocket and skidded across the sidewalk. No one bothered to pick it up. Then they drove off and I never saw him again. But somehow I had a feeling that he would be all right after all. A woman approached me and handed me a bottle of water and a sandwich. I drank the entire bottle and then I wolfed down that sandwich. But alas, it wouldn't stay down. I felt embarrassed but she told me not to worry. A while later she had another sandwich for me, but cautioned me to eat slowly and to chew well. This time it stayed down and I felt so much better.

Soon they were ready to pull up the adults. Aunt Anne came out first and then, one after another, all of the survivors were rescued. In daylight, I realized how pitiful and filthy we all looked, full of dust and caked mud. Everyone's clothes were an almost uniform grey and there were many crusted cuts and bruises on hands and faces. But we were the lucky ones. We had been in that awful prison for two and one half days and had miraculously survived. A head count revealed that twenty others had not been so lucky.

Everybody received a little something to eat and we now had plenty of water. I walked over and retrieved Hansi's car. I wanted to know whom to give it to so that Hansi would get it back. Nobody knew or even cared. I was told that I may keep it. It became one of my dearest possessions.

The ones that still had a home to go to went there to assess the damages. The others were picked up by a Red Cross bus and were taken to a shelter to be reunited with friends or relatives. For a while my thoughts went back over the trauma which we had just barely survived. As a child that had grown up knowing nothing but war, I couldn't react to all of this as perhaps an adult would, someone who could compare between war and how it used to be, or better yet, how it should be. I had heard so much about killed or missing soldiers, bombings and death that I thought it all to be quite normal, except that this time we had personally been involved in it. This, while it perhaps kept me and other children of my age from being too seriously affected by it all, nevertheless had caused us to become somewhat indifferent to the suffering of others. Some died while some survived; for the survivors life went on.

Aunt Anne and I were lucky once again. The portion of the building that contained her apartment was still standing. We went upstairs and were amazed how little damage had been done to her home. Several windows were broken from the blast and a thick coat of dust covered everything. Plaster hung from the ceiling of the living room, ripped off by flying shrapnel from the exploding bombs. I immediately looked for and secured several small bomb fragments. Boys of all ages collected these twisted bits of bombs and shells as treasured souvenirs. Now I had some of my own.

Phones were, for the moment, inoperative. No one could be reached. We just had to wait to call my mother. Aunt Anne busied herself with washing and wiping down her furniture, while I surveyed the neighborhood.

A typical city street scene, in the days following a bomb raid.

The changed panorama was overwhelming. Where large and impressive city houses and stores used to be, there was nothing but rubble left as far as the eye could see. An occasional chimney was still standing, reaching five stories tall into the nothingness of a grey afternoon sky. People were everywhere, searching, digging and some were weeping quietly. It soon became too much for me and I headed back to my aunt's place, one of the few sections of homes still standing. When I got there, she was upset and close to tears. She had again tried desperately to reach my mother but somewhere the lines were dead and no long distance calls could be made. I tried to calm her and told her that since my mother had no way of knowing what had happened here, there was no reason for her to worry much about us.

We finally were able to talk to Mother the next day. She said she could not come for me, so Aunt Anne took me to the railroad station and put me on a train for Munich. A large sign was hung around my neck with my name and address on it. It was a tearful good-bye and I remember being in no particular hurry to get home. Except for our ordeal with the bombing, I had really enjoyed my visit with Aunt Anne.

The train ride was slow and boring and after awhile the train stopped altogether in a field in the middle of nowhere. The other people in my compartment then heard a rumor that the locomotive had suffered a broken axle.

Destruction of tracks often caused damage to trains, which resulted in more delays.

I wanted to go up front and have a look, but my fellow passengers would not allow me to leave the compartment, since no one knew when the train might start running again. Five hours later, the whistle blew and we were off and on our way once more. Everyone was relieved to be moving again. It was said that passenger trains were a prime target for bombers and fighter planes as well. There were many more unscheduled stops and when we finally arrived in Munich we were seven hours late.

What little I could see of Munich, it looked even worse than the devastation I had witnessed in Stuttgart. Mother was glad to see me, but quite annoyed at the long wait. On the train ride to Starnberg I told her of our ordeal and she couldn't believe that we had come through as well as we did.

Soon, summer vacation was over and it was back to school for me. I couldn't wait to tell my class mates and my teachers about my experience in Stuttgart. The responses I got, however, were quite disappointing. Since these things were by then such a commonplace occurrence, no one really cared to hear about it. A shrug of the shoulders and "That's war, be thankful you're still alive," was the general reaction. I gradually realized that they were right and stopped talking about it so freely. A human life didn't mean much anymore unless it concerned one of your immediate family. Looking back on it all, I think it is such a shame how children, having the misfortune to grow up in such a turbulent and violent environment, became changed for the worse. They tended to lose respect for human life and became indeed hardened towards other people's feelings and sufferings.

Chapter Five

Death From Above

Due to a teachers' conference, our class was let out early one Thursday in October of 1944. We were told that there would be no classes for the next two days either. Hurray! No school till Monday. Arriving home, I pestered Mother to let me go to Munich to visit my grandparents for a couple of days. At first she had reservations because of the frequent bombing raids on the city.

"I can't let you go there," she tried to explain to me, "It's just no longer safe in the city. I don't want to lose you."

I was touched by her concern. It was rare for her to show her love and concerns about me openly and somehow I relished this rare occurrence.

I knew that what she said made sense. The nightmare of Stuttgart flashed through my mind, but I quickly pushed it aside. I was neither ready nor willing to dwell on that now. Then I remembered that it had been in October of 1943, relatively early in the war, that our apartment house in Munich had received severe bomb damage. Shortly thereafter, our automotive supply store was completely devastated.

*

Mentally, I started reliving these earlier experiences. At the age of eight, after our home in Munich had been destroyed, I had continued school in Starnberg. Because of the ever increasing bomb raids, we were quite happy to be far away from the city. In those days it had been mostly British bombers, like the Lancasters and Bristol Blenheims, that flew these missions. Later they were joined by American B-17s and even later by their B-24s as well.

My parents' business used to be on a major Munich thoroughfare only five minutes from where we used to live. It was a large automotive parts and supply store. It had been closed down by then due to lack of personnel. Besides, earlier, this main street had been turned into a major construction site. The city had started digging tunnels for a planned subway system. As the war progressed, however, the project had been abandoned for lack of funds and manpower. Motor traffic on this street had come to a complete halt, but these unfinished tunnels provided convenient bomb shelters for the neighborhood population.

Then it was early December 1943: To save our meager remaining stock of merchandise, my mother had organized a convoy of trucks and some laborers to evacuate the entire contents to our weekend place in Starnberg. Grandpa had refurbished some large storage sheds that were in the back of our property. These were now empty, awaiting delivery of our stock. It had been a tedious and tremendously costly undertaking to obtain these trucks and workers. Every palm wanted to be greased and many strings had to be pulled. But then, Mother had always been a great organizer. Finally one morning, the trucks were lined up and the men started to load.

At 1:00 p.m. there was an air alert. As the sirens were wailing, everybody dropped everything and ran down into the subway tunnel. For a long time we heard bombs falling all around us and smoke and dust started drifting through the passages. Eventually, we heard the "All Clear" sirens. As we returned, the store and

60

the five stories of apartments on top of it were partially on fire. As much as the tremendous heat allowed, the men commenced loading stock, that was still accessible, onto the trucks. The store front was still relatively cool and approachable, but the stockrooms to the rear were engulfed in flames and fumes. Barrel after barrel of engine oil and other assorted chemicals exploded in the heat, causing ever new infernos.

No one could believe it when, at 4:00 p.m., the sirens started wailing once more. Again, we scrambled for the subway and Mother and I huddled together in a corner. It was quite cold down there, after all it was winter. In no time, bombs rained down once again, this time the explosions seemed much louder and closer. When it was finally over, our building was no more.

The view was heartbreaking — December 1943.

There was nothing but a huge pile of rubble left of the entire six story structure. It must have received one or more direct hits with one of their new blockbuster bombs. The shock wave had blown out the

61

flames for the most part, but what was left was not worth rescuing. Cluster after cluster of bombs had screamed down onto the city, smashing row upon row of six story houses, collapsing overpasses, churning even our trucks into unrecognizable shapes. Now we had lost everything, but we were alive.

There seemed to be a major commotion farther down the street at the next subway entrance. Through side streets a few make-shift ambulances had appeared and were loading wounded children onto stretchers. While Mother was debating with our drivers, I walked over there to have a look. The first thing I noticed was a large crater in the middle of the road. Through it I could see right down into the subway tunnel. Wounded women and children writhed in agony or came crawling out of the crater, bleeding. Their cries and moans cut through me. But I tried to overcome it and, wanting to help, approached the hole. I was chased back by an old man who told me to go on home.

By coincidence I met a former classmate there. He still lived nearby and had come out to see if he could help. A survivor from the tunnel had told him that a choir teacher had brought her class of young girls to the subway, had led them down the many stairs and told them, "Here you are safe." She was wrong. They had been sitting right where the bomb hit. None of them survived. It became apparent later that one of the blockbusters had hit a ventilation duct, passed right through and gone on unimpeded into the overcrowded main tunnel. On hitting the tunnel floor it exploded, killing one hundred forty three old men, women and children and wounding at least twice that many.

On the grounds where the Oktoberfest used to be held there had been an anti aircraft gun installation.

It had consisted of countless 8.8 centimeter guns. These guns had been extremely effective, and had brought down many an enemy aircraft. To avoid the gunfire, the bombers had to fly so high that, during daytime raids, we could just see groups of silver specks against a background of blue sky. From that altitude precise hits on selected targets were coincidence at best. Then one night, as chance would have it, the entire gun installation was thoroughly wiped out during a night attack. Munich lay helpless and, for the most part unprotected, at the mercy of the bombers.

Allied Intelligence had to be working with astonishing accuracy, because from that day on the bombers arrived flying so low that we could easily make out their individual markings

Then once more, Stuttgart came to mind, again I suppressed it. But in spite of all this, I just had to see my grandparents again.

*

With my thoughts returning to the present, I still begged Mother to let me go.

"It won't be for long, Mom," I pleaded, "Only for a couple of days. Please!" Then finally she agreed. By train and by streetcar I arrived there unannounced; they had no telephone. But I knew I would be welcome there anytime. My relationship with my grandparents had always been something special.

I dearly loved both of them and I felt especially close to Grandpa. He was more than a father to me. He was six foot tall, portly built with friendly blue eyes, silvery hair and a handle-bar mustache. His witty humor made him very endearing; he was well liked by everyone. He was an avid hunter and had taken me along on many occasions, teaching me to hunt and also respect for the outdoors. Grandma was a warm, friendly woman, a little more reserved and quiet than Grandpa, but always generous, helpful, reliable and understanding. She wore her gray hair under a fine net with a little bun behind her head. Her glasses made her blue eyes appear larger than they were and she always wore ankle-long dresses.

They were delighted to see me, but Grandpa asked right away, "Are you skipping school, son?"

"No, Grandpa," I said, "there is teacher's conference and I couldn't wait to come and see you."

"And Mother allowed you to come in spite of the bombs?"

"It wasn't easy," I told him, "but I guess I was lucky and was able to talk her into letting me go."

"You must have been doing some fast talking," he grinned, "but I suppose you're quite good at that when you want something bad enough."

I thought it better not to respond to that but asked Grandma for a piece of cake instead. For the rest of that day we had a grand old time together.

That night, there were no bombs and we counted our blessings. The next morning around ten o'clock, however, the horrible ebbing and swelling wail of the "Air Raid" sirens started up across the city. My grandparents lived on the second floor of a four story house, directly over a passage way that connected the courtyard in the rear to the street out front. This was used mainly for delivery vehicles servicing the soft drink warehouse located in the back building. Grandma immediately grabbed her little emergency suitcase and the three of us went down to the basement.

Upon entering, I immediately remembered my recent experience in Stuttgart. I didn't want to be in that basement. I started walking around and soon found and explored several connecting passage ways. One of them ended at a heavy door which was unlocked. It led to the outside and over a flight of stairs into the back courtyard. Carefully closing the door again, I returned to where my grandparents were. I asked Grandpa's permission to explore the entire basement, thereby assuring that I wouldn't be missed prematurely. As soon as I was out of sight, I ran around the many corners to the door I had found earlier. Quietly I climbed up into the courtyard. Here I planned to wait for the "All Clear" sirens and then quickly join my grandparents, before I was missed.

In front of me loomed the passage. There were heavy double doors on each end of that passage. Both wings of the inner one were open while the one to the street was closed. I walked through the passageway to sneak a look outside. Slowly I opened the outer door partly and looked out into the deserted street. There was not a soul to be seen anywhere. The city was ghostly quiet. It was by now close to eleven o'clock and there was not a cloud in the sky.

Gradually I began to hear an ominous droning sound from above. Then there were the first explosions in the distance. The droning became thunderous as it came closer and now I could see several bomber squadrons appearing in the sky from the south. As they came nearer, the bombs dropping down from them became plainly visible. Now the planes were overhead. I did not want to be buried again so I was just trying to run out into the street. Looking up, I froze. A huge bomb came spiraling down until it disappeared behind the roof top of the house across the street. There was a blinding orange colored flash as it hit.

The shockwave tore the air out of my lungs, picked me up and threw me clear through the entire passage, enveloping me in a cloud of debris and dust. Dazed, I found I had been slammed into one of the prickly bushes of the inner courtyard forty-five feet away. My ears were ringing but I thought that the explosions were receding to the north of us. And then it was quiet once again. Slowly I untangled myself from those scratchy branches and looked around. I still felt dizzy. The doors next to the courtyard were undamaged. The ones to the street had been blown off their hinges but looked to be still in one piece. I walked through the passage and through the opening.

Dust clouds hanging in the air were making it difficult to perceive anything clearly. I leaned against a wall behind me and waited for the dust to settle and for my ears to quit ringing somewhat. After awhile the ringing actually subsided and most of the dust had settled. Now I couldn't believe what I saw when I looked out into the street. Two thirds of the house across the street was gone. A pile of rubble reached up to the second floor level of the portion still standing. The inside of the rooms of the upper three floors were now visible from the street. The missing wall, no longer affording any privacy, showed all the different interior colors people had used to decorate their rooms. On the third floor I saw an old woman sitting in a rocking chair. She was still alive. Every once in a while, debris crumbled off the roof, landing on the top floor or tumbling all the way down onto the pile of rubble. Now I saw flames belching from the remaining roof structure. Someone started screaming frantically.

I turned and slunk back down into the basement before I would be missed. My attempts to join them unnoticed, however, failed completely. My grandparents saw me come in. Even by the dim light of the customary blue light bulb I noticed their expressions change to horror.

"Where have you been?" they both yelled.

At first I couldn't figure what could have given me away. Too late I realized my obvious appearance. From the top of my head to the tips of my shoes I was covered by a uniform shade of grey dust. I looked like someone had dumped a sack of cement over me, as Grandpa later put it. Grandma wiped my face with her apron and revealed bleeding scratches from the prickly bush. It was time to confess.

"I didn't want to be in this basement," I whined, "I'm sorry!"

They had known about my experience in Stuttgart and tried hard to understand my foolish behavior. Just then the long awaited "All Clear" sirens could be heard throughout the city. I was off the hook.

As we went upstairs, my grandparents first went out into the street to see what had happened. There was still not a cloud in the sky, but standing out in the open, we did not have a shadow. The sun was obliterated by a brownish-grey haze that hung over our part of the city. Fires were burning everywhere. Distressed survivors with no place to go ran around aimlessly, carrying with them a few precious belongings.

We went upstairs. Dust was everywhere. The windows to the front and to the rear were blown out. That meant all their windows were gone since there were no windows or even exposed walls to the sides. These city houses were all built against each other without any gaps between them. Other than that, no damage was done. I was amazed how calmly my Grandparents took that mess in stride. It turned out that this was not the first time it had happened, it had just become increasingly more difficult to get someone to replace the glass. Grandma cleaned me up as well as possible and gave me a bowl of soup. Grandpa didn't want anything. He said he would look into getting the glass replaced and invited me to come with him.

As we walked toward the nearest thoroughfare, we could see the extent of the damage to the next parallel street. Entire city blocks had been laid to waste with nothing left standing on either side of the streets. All that could be seen were some nearby, lonesome looking chimneys and, farther in the distance, the blackened remains of torn and gutted buildings.

Upon reaching the main street, we saw that there had been little effort at cleanup as yet. From the looks of it the rubble had just been pushed out of tracks of the streetcars. Some of it was still smoldering. Grandpa didn't say much anymore. His usually cheery disposition had vanished somewhere a few streets back. At one corner was a tram stop, relatively undamaged. We went in and I heard Grandpa inquire about the connections to Starnberg, my home. Apparently the news was good, so he bought a ticket for me. He put me on the tram, assuring me that he and Grandma would be quite all right. I guess he wanted me out of the way.

After the dust had settled, these lonely chimneys came into view.

At the main railroad station I had to transfer to a commuter train which would take me home. Luck was with me, a train was just ready to leave for Garmisch, the renowned ski resort and Starnberg was a station-stop on that route. It was by now 4:30 p.m. I squeezed in with the usual commuter crowd but had to stand out on an open platform. The wind was bitter cold, but I huddled amongst the coats of the people that were stacked like sardines. This helped me over the worst chill. Whole droves of people were even riding on the step boards, hanging on to handrails. They took the brunt of the draft. I didn't envy them. Of course, people were used to travelling like that by now, but it didn't do much for their dispositions.

Suddenly we came to an unscheduled stop between two stations. The train had just left the outskirts of the city, passing into one of Munich's western suburbs. There was another air raid alarm, the second one that day. Passengers were ordered by the conductor to crawl under the train. Most of them did, but some ran to a nearby ditch and hid themselves as well as possible. A few remained inside the compartments, thereby securing themselves a seat for the remainder of the trip if it would still come to that. I stayed where I was. I didn't want to be under anything and I certainly didn't want to be left behind.

When the attack came, it turned out to be a minor one. Still, it came closer than hoped for. The bombers were only about a mile away when they started dropping their deadly cargo. All alone I stood on the platform of the last car and watched through the smoke and dust as rubble blew skyward under the bombers barrage. Then it became clear to me what their target must be. Only a mile behind us, there was a gigantic bridge spanning the many tracks of the railroad. Over it went a main thoroughfare to the city. I watched as the rain of bombs reached the bridge and engulfed it in smoke and dust. When the smoke cleared, the bridge lay in ruins, torn and ripped into a mangled mess of twisted steel and shattered concrete. Every train-track in and out of the city from that direction was utterly blocked by the wreckage.

Soon thereafter came the "All Clear" sirens and everyone rushed back onto the train. I had a head-start and got inside before the crowd. There were still empty seats but I didn't dare sit while adults would be standing. I was glad to at least be inside for the remainder of the trip. People discussed how lucky we had been that the train had already passed through that bridge, before it was annihilated. We would have all been stranded in Munich. There were no further incidents and I arrived at home safely. As much as I loved my grandparents, I had lost any desire to return to the city anytime soon.

As the war neared its disastrous conclusion, the attacks on Munich and just about all other German cities had drastically increased not only in numbers but especially in ferocity. Squadrons of Flying Fortresses kept flying low along city streets, blanketing the large apartment houses on both sides with their blockbuster bombs. They were cruising just high enough to be safe from the explosions below. This happened during daylight as well as at nights. Schools and hospitals seemed to be the prime targets. The accepted custom of painting a large Red Cross symbol on the roof of hospitals soon had to be abandoned. These symbols had turned into preferred marks for the bombers.

Many times at night, Mother and I would walk down to our pier on the lake. We were about twenty miles south of Munich but all too often the entire northern horizon could be seen blood-red, interspersed with bright yellow flashes and flare-ups. Munich, my hometown, was burning once again.

We knew of some "regulars," fire-watchers, who never missed a chance to come out and observe the horrible displays caused by these infernos. Later, statistics available after the end of the war, told of a total of some 16,000 such fire storms over Munich alone.

Chapter Six

The "Enemy"

It was the latter part of April 1945, when conflicting reports about the imminent defeat of Germany started coming over the radio. One of them came from a station installed to give current air raid information. Some well known Nazi leaders had switched loyalties and exposed to the population the ghastly extent of collapse of the German army on all fronts. The futility of any hope for a last minute turnaround was openly explained on the air. They advised the German people not to resist the advance of the enemy in any way. Hints were made that secret agreements with the Allied Forces had been devised so no further destruction of Germany would be forthcoming if Germany surrendered speedily and unconditionally. In order to save lives and property, everyone was urged to comply with that directive.

Only hours later, this broadcast was retracted on the regular local radio station. The orchestrators of that earlier newscast were denounced as criminals and traitors. The public again was ordered under threat of death to defend the Fatherland to their last breath and to report anyone not complying with this to the Nazi authorities. We were told that the traitorous instigators had been rounded up and executed for treason.

It didn't take long and these supposedly executed former Nazis were on the air at the other station once again, pleading to let common sense prevail and to do nothing that would only prolong the agony of a hopeless situation. And so it went back and forth. We had known that the end was near but no one knew what to expect. No one could be certain of what would become of us. Nazi propaganda had never missed an opportunity to brainwash the population about the enemy's character. We had been told that the GIs were all a bunch of hardened criminals, let out of prison to fight as Allied soldiers. That if we surrendered, they would hang us from the nearest tree and much worse. Of course any halfway intelligent person could see this for what it was, propaganda of the simplest kind. We knew that the average soldier on either side only did what he was ordered to do and would much rather be at home with his loved ones pursuing a normal and peaceful life. Now, all we could do was hope and pray for the best.

On the afternoon of April 30, 1945, Mother and I had gone into town to try and get some last minute food supplies. The outcome had been even more meager than expected. Everyone was quite nervous with the contemplation of our unknown fate. What was on everybody's mind was Hitler's order from March 19, 1945, stating that every town is to be *defended to the last man*. And then the latest of Hitler's order from March 30, 1945, *only scorched soil is to be left to the enemy*. The people knew that the various SS fighting units, stationed near Starnberg would force the population to help them defend our town to the last man. Several Volkssturm members, not agreeing with these SS orders, had actually been shot, on the spot. Allied Intelligence was, of course, aware of the presence of these SS units and their fanatic intentions. U.S. troops, surrounding Starnberg, were ready and willing to annihilate the town at the first sign of armed resistance. And we, the German civilian population, were caught in the middle, trembling for our lives.

Before walking home, we stopped by the house of some friends. They were an elderly couple. The man had built an addition to our little house and since then he did odd jobs or cut and split firewood for us, whenever needed.

His name was Mr. Kern. He was about seventy-five years old. His hair was still surprisingly dark for his age, but one rarely got to see it, he always wore a hat. He had friendly, blue eyes and he possessed a generous amount of whimsical humor. His mouth was crooked because there was always a big, long pipe dangling from it and always from the same corner. He'd suck on it if it was lit or not, but mostly it was cold for want of tobacco. The sheer weight of it, over the years, had drawn the right side of his mouth down considerably and whenever he removed the pipe while speaking, eating or sleeping, his mouth stayed at its odd angle.

His wife was a frail little woman of about eighty-one who walked acutely bent over so that when she talked to me her face was at the same level with mine. Her snow-white hair was worn in a tight bun behind her head. She was endowed with a brilliant intelligence and could recite hour-long poems without any hesitation. They both had always been very friendly and helpful.

Their small house bordered Main Street and whenever we did our shopping, we would park our packages and bags at their place so we wouldn't have to drag them all over town to the next store. Then, when we had all our stuff together, we would begin the twenty-five minute walk to our home outside of town.

It had been in October of 1944, that fanatic Nazi leaders such as Himmler, Borman and others had given the order to create an organization which they called Volkssturm, which, freely translated, meant Public Defence. It called for all remaining old men, women and even children to defend the Fatherland to the last drop of blood. The population, however, perceived it as "the last roundup of the old and the lame, the children and the dotards." The military had then ordered caches of weapons and ammunition to be buried in fields and forests. They were to be dug up and used for that last defence.

By now, however, the active Nazis had all gone into hiding and the German population had no desire to prolong the agony of war. People well remembered the nights of November 22, 1944 and again of December 17. They had seen more than 1000 American B-17 bombers, along with their fighter escorts, collecting themselves over our lake in preparation for another attack on residential areas of Munich. By the end of 1944, Munich had been reduced to a pile of rubble. On April 29, 1945, only yesterday, a throng of U.S. dive bombers had again rendezvoused over the lake during the early morning hours and ultimately headed towards Munich where they probably provided the city's "death dance". Yes, the people were thoroughly fed up with war. Especially in view of news reports about the severity of the recent bomb raids on other German civilian targets.

The people were still shocked to hear what had happened in Dresden on February 14, and 15, 1945:

This quaint and beautiful, medieval city, located in central Germany, had at that time been choked with untold multitudes of German civilian refugees. They had been on their way westward, fleeing from the advancing Russian army. Due to the destruction of the railways these people were hopelessly bottle-necked in this city. The Allies had known about this and in February 1945, England's Winston Churchill had ordered a massive air raid on Dresden that lasted two days. There had never been any war industry or military targets in this lovely, peaceful, old city.

Here are some details as they were revealed to us on a later date:

It had started with seven-hundred-seventy-three British Lancaster bombers dropping 2700 tons of bombs. First, T.N.T. bombs to destroy the roofs and blast out the windows of the houses. Then they dropped 650,000 incendiary bombs which created fire-storms of an unimaginable ferocity. These fire-storms then swept through the city, utterly destroying everything and everybody in it. Only hours later, 311 American B-17 bombers continued with this depraved massacre and dropped another 771 tons of bombs. The next day, American B-17s again attacked the, by then completely ruined, city.

Some of the bodies of the victims were reduced to the size of a loaf of bread and completely blackened by the tremendous heat. Official estimates of people killed reached two hundred forty-five thousand, all of them helpless, innocent civilians. (This amounts to many more than what later would perish from both atom-bombs combined!) Dresden was completely destroyed and did not even begin to function again until at least a year after the end of the war.

Dresden, after the first day of raids. There was nothing left to
photograph, after the second day of raids — February 1945.

Before that, the German people had felt that bombings were done to invoke terror on the population and
wear down their willingness to keep fighting, as if we
civilians ever had any desire to fight. But what
happened to Dresden became a gruesome example of
the ferocity of the enemy and was no longer seen as
just normal warfare. It was perceived clearly as what
it was, premeditated mass-murder. But now the people
were so glad it would finally all be over, that they would
do nothing but watch and wave as the invading GIs
started marching down Main Street.

As we sat with the old couple and speculated about
our uncertain future, the first American troops could
be seen marching into town. Thanks to God, there was
no fighting. As we found out later, intense negotia-
tions between SS unit leaders, Nazi big-shots and

fanatic Fatherland defenders on one hand and the Bürgermeister, the priest and war-tired civilian leaders on the other hand, had finally been successful in preventing any hostile actions against the approaching Americans. But there were no guarantees. Reports still drifted in of high ranking SS officers shooting German civilians that were caught hoisting white flags upon public buildings.

But now, the enemy had arrived. To me it was an eerie sensation. Somehow they seemed like an army of ghosts. We could hear no noise from their rubber-soled combat boots. The racket from the German soldier's hobnailed boots that we were so used to was utterly missing. Also, the netting on their helmets was new to us, since we were used to only seeing the German's shiny steel helmets.

Individual U.S. soldiers checked each house and asked if there were any German soldiers hiding out. Of course, there were none now. Earlier, scores of retreating German soldiers had been knocking on the doors of civilians, begging for old civilian clothing which they quickly exchanged for their uniforms before they quietly vanished. The rest of Germany's soldiers were all at the various front lines, or dead, or taken prisoner by now.

A detail went into town hall to round up and arrest all the officials that were still there. The active Nazis had all disappeared. However, most of them were routed out one by one in the weeks and months to come. As they were found, they were put into detention camps. Much later it became known that after the inmates of the concentration camps had been liberated by Allied troops, these camps, such as Buchenwald, with their very same facilities, were then used to house Nazi party members until the de-nazification process was completed.

On the suggestion of the old lady, Mr. Kern offered to walk home with us and spend the night. She figured Mother and I needed the protection of a man more than she would, being eighty-one years old. We were touched, but Mother declined. She told them that she thought we would be all right. If not, there was nothing we or he could do about it.

We arrived at home without incident. We lived on a secondary road which went around the entire lake. So far there was no military traffic on secondary roads. That came later that night. After a meager evening meal, we closed our shutters, shut off all the lights and went to bed.

All night the drone of heavy equipment and tanks was heard from the distant main highway. And later, even on our road huge tanks, trucks and canons passed intermittently all through the night. They rode in darkness and only occasionally a small position light could be seen. Some accidently drifted off the road in the darkness and rolled over fences, shrubs and whatever else stood in their way. Several heavy tanks drove through a row of greenhouses belonging to the nearby nursery, scattering glass shards everywhere.

The next morning, May 1, my 10th birthday, American soldiers were everywhere. All along the lake shore people were being evicted from their homes to make room for the troops. The owner of the mansion next door to us had been spared from the draft. The factory that he owned near Munich was producing material important to the military. He was known as a fast talking manipulator and spoke English fluently. It didn't take him long to convince the American commanding officer of our area to let his family remain in their home (an expensive Leica camera did a lot of convincing.)

In exchange, he would take in several of the neighboring families from houses that were now occupied by the troops.

They also came to the little house Mother and I lived in. My father had bought the seven-acre waterfront property in 1939 as a weekend retreat. It was located about a mile south of the town of Starnberg. Starnberg is about twenty miles south of Munich. The main house was an old, stately mansion, rented out to tenants. Father wasn't interested in that. There had been a little two-room outbuilding which he had completely refurbished and converted into a cozy little weekend cottage for us. It was a small house with white stucco covering the outside and with red fluted tiles on the roof. The two rooms inside were modest but comfortable and attractively furnished. As a weekend retreat it was large enough. Then, in October of 1943, when our residence in Munich was destroyed by bombs, Mother and I stayed in this tiny house permanently. Mother had found a local, retired brick mason who added a small kitchen and a bathroom to our two original rooms. Now she could cook properly and we no longer had to use that old outhouse that Grandpa had built for us in the rear of our property.

As the soldiers came to our little abode, we showed them in and asked them if we really had to leave as well. We pointed out the small size of the house. They said they would ask their captain and let us know. Then we waited, but no one came. Uncertain of what would happen, Mother told me to start carrying bedding and other essentials to our neighbor's mansion. On my way there I had to pass our main house, it was already full of soldiers. There were trucks and Jeeps with trailers parked on the driveway and at the little walk-through gate there were more soldiers standing around. One leaned on a gatepost with a pistol in his hands, another one near the other post was eating what looked like white pudding out of a can. I had my arms full of pillows and blankets and had to pass between them. The hand with the gun, while not exactly pointed at me, was in my way. I forced a smile on my face, and gently pushed his arm, gun and all aside and with trembling steps I walked by him, wishing I was a hundred miles away. I heard laughing behind me and some remarks in English which I didn't understand, but I resisted the urge to turn around to see if I would be shot. I would have been far more interested in that pudding. When I returned, the gun was nowhere to be seen and the can was empty. The soldiers grinned at me and let me pass. Out of sight, I heaved a mighty sigh of relief.

Later, the captain himself did come to look at our home. His name was Captain Ansbach and in passable German he asked a few questions which we answered truthfully. He was a tall, slender man with a ruddy complexion. His grey hair was clipped to a crewcut and when he talked, I could watch his Adam's-apple bob up and down against the skin of his neck. His manner of talking to us seemed rather reserved. He acted politely and he did not appear arrogant, but we thought we could detect a deliberate remoteness in his voice, especially at first. We did not feel offended, however, after all, we thought, he was the enemy. Finally, his manner became more cordial and he told us that we could stay. We would, however, have to take in a young woman with her five year old girl. We were glad, at least we could stay in our house. Mother thanked the captain and told him that it was my birthday and that she had baked a cake for me. She invited him to come over and help us celebrate in the afternoon. She apologized that there would be no coffee since she didn't have any. Captain Ansbach thanked her but did not commit himself.

I went over to the neighbor's house again and retrieved all of our bedding. We got our little home back in order while the soldiers settled into the big house. Word about my birthday must have gotten around, however, because later that day several other soldiers showed up with a large pot of steaming hot coffee. Coffee! Coffee in those days, was an unobtainable commodity; all we were able to get was imitation coffee made from malt or barley, or God knows what else. We therefore really appreciated this treasure and were happy to see that the soldiers thoroughly enjoyed Mother's cake. One of those soldiers was the one with the gun. He laughed as he recognized me and told my mother in his broken German that I was a very brave boy. Even though a certain shyness still prevailed, we had a wonderful afternoon together. But in the following days, due to their order not to socialize with civilians, and also partly due to our shyness, we stayed out of each other's way and thus got along just fine.

It was much later, that we learned about a directive from the U.S. Military Chiefs of Staff, dated April 26, 1945, prohibiting any fraternizing of U.S. troops with the German population. It said specifically that Germany had not been occupied for the purpose of liberation but as an enemy that had lost the war. As such, Germans are to be dealt with correctly, but never-the-less in accordance of a stern occupational regime.

During the second night, there was a commotion at the neighbor's place. In the rear portion of his property, a large warehouse stood hidden amongst the trees. He had been renting it to the Nazis for the storage of emergency equipment and various supplies, to be used in any major disaster. Our neighbor, of course, now looked at these as his personal property. From back there came some noises, a woman screamed and then we heard a shot. We didn't dare go out and look, but through our open window we heard people running back and forth. No one ever openly talked about what had happened. However, it was rumored that a former inmate of a concentration camp, recognizable by the black and white striped outfit he still wore, had broken into that warehouse. When one of the women next door checked out the noise, he had tried to rape her. His body was found the next day on the nearby railroad tracks, decapitated by one of the few trains that occasionally still came through.

It had been right after the invasion, that some high ranking American officer declared Munich and the surrounding country side an "open area" and permitted these former concentration camp inmates to rob, rape, murder, plunder and burn to their heart's content without any fear of reprisals. However, most of them were hardened criminals. The German people were petrified with fear about this new threat and many remembered the often repeated Nazi propaganda about the evil intentions of the enemy, wondering if these predictions were about to come true after all. The unspeakable atrocities inflicted on the innocent population at the hands of these unscrupulous convicts and depraved criminals defy any description. All appeals of the German public to American authorities to stop this shameful scandal fell on deaf ears. They justified their refusal to intervene with the lame excuse that all this had been a long planned scheme by a certain faction of the Allies. After three days of unchecked mayhem, however, the American authorities finally recognized the lunacy of that arrangement and quickly put a stop to it.

Then one night, we awoke from a great noise in the front house. A loud and wild party seemed to be going on in there and it lasted almost until daybreak. But the soldiers kept to themselves and didn't bother anybody. The next morning we found about thirty empty wine bottles, along with the straw jackets they had been wrapped in, scattered behind the house. Mother looked at them and thought she recognized the labels. She got the key for the woodshed, called for me and together we went to check it out.

Farther back on our property there were some old wooden buildings. After my father had bought the place, my grandfather repaired and made them usable once again. This way we had a dry space for all kind of odds and ends. Mainly we had stored excess furniture from our Munich apartment in anticipation of bomb damage. As it turned out these were all that we had been able to salvage from our household in the city. Some excess warehouse stock from my parents' automotive parts and accessory store were also hidden there. But alas, not nearly enough.

We found the hasp on each door broken and the doors hung half open. With ill feelings we started to check what was missing. Of the furniture, the locked doors and drawers had been forced open, but all that seemed to be missing was the wine. There used to be about thirty bottles of expensive wine that were stored in one of the wardrobes. These were gone now.

Cameras, binoculars, typewriters and other valuables, however, were untouched. We were grateful. They had taken the wine and obviously had had a good time, but no one was hurt. The amazing thing to us was that they had not touched any of our belongings. We very much respected them for that. Together we fixed the hasps and locked the sheds once again. The soldiers knew by now that we knew, but neither we nor they ever mentioned it. There were still a few bottles of that wine that Mother had kept in the house. They would come in handy later on.

After a couple of weeks, many trucks and personnel carriers showed up. There was a lot of running back and forth amongst the soldiers, as equipment was being moved, loaded and unloaded. The activities reminded me of a busy bee hive. Then someone said that the troops were being replaced by other soldiers. The invasion troops we had seen so far had been part of the 7th and 9th US Army armored tank divisions. Now, they were being replaced by troops belonging to the US 3rd Army. These new soldiers would be the occupation troops and would stay on for an indefinite period of time. As the transition progressed, we just stayed out of the way. By now we knew we had nothing to fear from the enemy, so we weren't overly concerned. We all considered ourselves lucky to be living in what had become the American Occupation Zone.

Chapter Seven

The Friend

After the invasion troops had moved on, the occupation troops swiftly settled in. Housing was rearranged once again. While most of the lake-front mansions were kept for the soldiers, certain smaller and older homes were freed to house the displaced and overcrowded locals. Our big house had been vacated and the original tenants had moved back in along with another German family from a nearby mansion. The young lady and her little daughter that had stayed with us had moved on to Munich to live with relatives.

In the big house next door, the owners had to move into the upper levels along with some of the remaining German families from occupied homes. On the main floor the soldiers installed a field kitchen and the troops were fed from there. A glimmer of hope appeared for us to perhaps be able to get some of their leftovers at times. But there was no chance to go there uninvited and wait for a handout. The GIs were still under orders not to mingle with the population and our enterprising neighbor, for reasons of his own, did not want any outsiders on his property.

My mother had forbidden that I should beg and I was too bashful to ask for anything. But many times I would wait at our side of the fence to say "Hi" to a passing soldier and smile at them. There was almost always a friendly response and once in a while I ended up with a piece of gum or even a candy bar.

It was a couple of days after the invasion troops had left that I walked down to our pier. An unexpected surprise awaited me there. Wherever I looked along our shoreline, countless boats of every description were dimpling in the calm water. Some were stranded on shore. Apparently the soldiers had taken these boats out from the various boat houses, used them and failed to secure them when they were ordered to move on. The prevailing wind had collected all of them on our western shore.

I was ecstatic. There was actually gasoline in the tanks of the motor boats, a commodity unavailable to the average German citizen for years. These boats had spent the last several years in their moorings for want of fuel. The soldiers apparently had filled the tanks, got the engines running once again and had fun. Most important now — there was fuel left in most of them as I soon found out. The various rowboats, dinghies and sailboats were of little interest to me as long as there were motorboats with fuel in their tanks. I ran around the neighborhood, invited a couple of buddies and soon we were racing up and down the lakes in these abandoned crafts. We hadn't had that much fun in a long time. As the fuel gauges approached the empty mark, we would come in to look for another boat. The wind, gentle as it was, had packed them so tightly that we were able to jump from one boat to the next in search of another one with fuel left in it. When evening came and we had to go home, we secured the motorboats that still had fuel to our pier. For this we used rope ends and lines from the sailboats. We also kept a number of sail boats. Row boats and motorboats with empty fuel tanks were of no further concern, so they were set adrift once again. For a couple of days we were happily busy playing "Captain", exchanging and racing boats of every kind and description and also teaching ourselves to handle sailboats in the process. Gradually, however, the new GIs secured most of the boats for their own use, but we had had the time of our lives while it lasted.

*

As I was standing at our fence one morning, watching the activities of the field kitchen, one of the soldiers came over towards me. He was a tall man, wearing army fatigues and a white T-shirt. His brown hair was combed straight back from his sun-tanned face. He looked to be in his late thirties. A big, friendly smile was on his face when he asked me in almost flawless German if this is where I lived. I told him that this was so and we chatted for quite awhile. His name was John Sonn and he worked as a helper in that kitchen. Then he asked me to meet him at around 6:00 p.m. at the back fence of our yard.

When the time came I sat at the back fence, screened by shrubs, waiting. It didn't take long and he came through the bushes looking for me. He carried an old cardboard box which he handed over the fence. I thanked him and wanted to talk but he was in a rush to get back before he was missed. Happily, I lugged the heavy box towards our house, taking great care not to be seen. I slipped through the door where Mother was waiting. Together we opened it and were overjoyed by what we found. There was a small sack of sugar, some flour, two Hershey bars, a pack of cigarettes, a can of butter, a can of coffee beans and a bar of soap. We were delighted and Mother tried to figure out what we could give in return to show our gratitude.

All the next morning I hung around near our fence, hoping to see Mr. Sonn. He had offered to be called Johnny but at my young age it just didn't seem right to address adults by their first names. When I finally spied him taking out some trash I thanked him again for everything and asked him when he could meet me back there in the bushes.

"I've got something for you, Mr. Sonn," I said in a low voice, "but I don't want to be seen." "That's not necessary," he replied smiling, "but I can be there in an hour."

When I told Mother, she wrapped one of the remaining bottles of expensive wine in an old newspaper and handed it to me. When I met him at the fence in the back, I gave him the wine and he handed me a brown paper bag. What I liked about him from the start was that he was always smiling and forever seemed to be in a happy mood. He thanked me for the wine with a big grin that showed off his white and amazingly even teeth. I also thanked him for the bag and wanted to talk. But he was in a hurry again and said he had to sneak back. He flashed another happy smile and was gone. The bag contained some cookies, two bars of soap and several packs of matches.

The next day, we heard someone banging on our bedroom window. Mother was startled and didn't know what to make of it. Then she told me to look and see what was going on. I opened the window and there was Mr. Sonn. He handed a large metal pot up to me and, with a twinkle in his eye, said he would need it back when it was empty. Smiling as always, he jumped the fence and was gone. There was a lot of vanilla pudding left in that pot and Mother and I both enjoyed this long forgotten extravagance.

Soon, the soldiers realized that their orders not to mix with the population were not at all seriously enforced. They started to talk to us more openly and slowly most of us had lost most of our shyness towards the "enemy".

We met many nice soldiers. Some of them, we soon realized, were quite homesick and told us much of their homeland and their way of life back in the States and couldn't wait to get back home. Others loved the Army life, since they really had not much to come home to once the service discharged them. Soon enough it became clear to us that these soldiers, even though they spoke a different language, were basically no different than we were. Most of them, however, did seem to me to be more easy going and friendlier than most of our own nervous and war-strained people.

*

For several days I had been hearing noisy activity and machinery at work at the nearby railway. One afternoon it ceased. The next day, I wanted to see what had been going on up there. I followed a gravel road that led to a bridge over the railway. Looking down from the bridge, I couldn't believe what I saw, the scene looked so weird. Where there used to be two tracks side by side, there was now only one. The other rails and the cross-ties had been completely removed. Later on I found out that what I had seen was part of the initial process of dismantling Germany, to secure war debts.

Apparently, as early as September 2, 1944, Henry Morgenthau, U.S. President F. D. Roosevelt's Jewish Minister of Finance, had had the sinister obsession of eradicating Germany completely once and for all. He had submitted a plan for the total and complete dismantling of all of German's industries, including the flooding of our mines. This evil plan further proposed to turn Germany into a purely pastoral society, with the population to be fed from soup kitchens. Germany was to be put under a penalty peace with Allied occupation. More than one-third of the German homeland was to be given to other, neighboring countries. The remaining part of Germany was to be split into two separate states with no political or economic significance. And for many decades to come, the German economy was to be kept under the tightest control.

On September 11, this "Morgenthau Plan" had been discussed at a meeting between Roosevelt and England's Churchill in Quebec. Roosevelt had wholeheartedly agreed with the plan and, after some reservations, so had Churchill, who was at that time expecting a sizeable U.S. credit to rebuild England. On September 21, however, details of this plan had leaked to the American public which, for the most part, responded with outrage. U.S. War minister Henry Lewis Stimson called the plan "a capital crime against civilization". On September 22, in view of elections only seven weeks ahead, Roosevelt withdrew his signature.

Thanks to the wise foresight of the American Chief of Staff, General George Catlitt Marshall, however, this did not happen. At least not in the western part of Germany which was now controlled by the Allies. General Marshall showed and finally convinced the United States Congress that no gain could ever be expected from a nation so crippled. With Marshall's idea of financially helping Germany to get back on its feet, Germany would be able not only to repay the initial costs of the "Marshall Plan", as it became known, but would in the long run be able to pay the tremendous reparation cost of the war. General Marshall counted on the diligence and ingenuity of the hard working German population and history later has proved him right. This highly perceptive and visionary general turned out to be a most genuine friend of the German people. To my knowledge, Germany is the only country that was able to repay in full all of its war debts.

*

Available boats had by now become scarce on the lake. Most of them had found their way back to their original owners and the rest were being used by the troops during their time off duty. One sunny day, Mother and I were just having lunch, Mr. Sonn came and invited Mother and me for a boat ride on the lake. He had secured a large row boat and had brought some sandwiches and soft drinks from his kitchen. There was only one pair of oars, so he had to do all the rowing by himself. We followed the shoreline south to the next village a few miles down the lake, with me jumping over the side and swimming along for a while whenever I felt like it. Once there, we tied the boat to an old pier and had a second lunch. On the way back, I tried my luck with rowing but the oars in that large boat were so far apart that I didn't accomplish much and soon handed them back to Mr. Sonn.

Many a happy day went by where we played together, joked around and had fun whenever he could get away or had a day off. I was delighted and wished it would never end. But then, one evening, Mr. Sonn came over and by his somber expression we knew that something was wrong. He told us that he would soon be leaving for the United States. Their detachment was scheduled to be dissolved and most of the men would be sent home and discharged from the service. He stayed a while and chatted but Mr. Sonn did not smile much that day. When he left, he motioned me outside, saying he had a present for me. I followed him through the stand of tall pines that surrounded our pond and there he showed me a paddle boat. It was a three-seater that could be disassembled and he told me it was mine. I was delighted and could hardly believe in my good luck. Unfortunately, as it turned out, it didn't last long. I never used it on the lake because I had no idea where he had gotten it from. I kept it out of sight, locked in a shed at nights. When I had the chance, I paddled it around the island in our private pond. One rainy evening though, I forgot to put it away. It was gone the next morning.

Chapter Eight

How Daddy Came Back

Dad had been drafted into service the very first day of the war. By necessity, he had been a member of the Nazi party. To obtain a license for any kind of enterprise, one had to be a member of the N.S.D.A.P., the National Social German Worker's Party. It was the only legally remaining party by then. But Dad had never been animated. In the eyes of some active Nazis, Dad, as the owner of a large, flourishing business, had not contributed enough to the party. So they kind of had it in for him.

I still faintly remember the night of September 1, 1939. Around midnight, Mom and our maid woke me to say "Good-bye" to Daddy and explained that he had to go to war. I barely could open my eyes and with my little hands I waved "Good-bye" to him and fell asleep immediately. I was four years old, I didn't understand. The next day, Dad was gone. Dad was in his late thirties then, of medium build with black hair and brown eyes. His glasses magnified his eyes some, which I always had found intriguing. He was an excellent businessman and while Mother was the soul of the business, Dad had been the brain.

After basic training at boot camp, he was sent to an anti-aircraft installation, at the western front. There, he hurt his leg in a fall and was shipped back to a military hospital near Stuttgart. Mom and I were able to visit him there once.

From left: Aunt Anne, Dad, Mom and author
with Dad's cap (in front,) while visiting Dad
at a hospital near Stuttgart — Spring of 1940.

According to one of Hitler's special directives, anyone who had participated in the first World War would be immediately advanced to the rank of a noncommissioned officer. Dad had served in that war for only three weeks, but that was enough to qualify. After his recovery he was transferred to an airport of the Luftwaffe, the German Air Force, near Stuttgart. He was promoted to second lieutenant, and assigned to administrative duty. Soon afterwards he advanced to first lieutenant and served as pay master for several years. In those days, Dad would regularly come home on leave. Then, in January of 1944, he was transferred to northern Italy.

Daddy, shortly before his transfer to Italy — October 1943.

We heard nothing from him after that. This was a very difficult and unnerving time for my mother.

On a cold and drizzly day in January of 1945, Mother told me to come along to see this elderly woman who practiced astrology. She had a reputation of being astonishingly accurate in her predictions. Mom was desperate and needed some hope. I had perceived that trip as a waste of time, but was nevertheless intrigued by this venture into the mysterious and the unknown. To obtain results, however, required a second trip. A horoscope would have to be created and evaluated. "Right!" I remember thinking, but I had kept my mouth shut.

To me, that old woman had looked close to what children imagined a witch would look like, or at least someone that wanted to create the impression of being

97

one. She was rough spoken and her manners left much to be desired. I didn't trust her. She ushered us into her back bedroom and sat down at a desk. Mom and I were offered to sit on the bed. After long and awkward explanations of moons, stars, houses and phases, she told Mom that Dad was alive but would be severely wounded. She mumbled something about a house of death, but foretold that he would, in time, come back home alive.

That was all Mom had needed. On our way home, she was in tears from worrying. I wished that we had never gone there. As Mom carried on, I finally told her not to believe all that mumbo-jumbo, and for nothing better to say I blurted out, "Why don't you ask her when the world will end, she can't know that either."

To my great surprise, this seemed to make sense to her or at least she desperately grasped at it as a way out of her misery.

"You know," she said to me, "you're right. She wouldn't know the answer to that. So how could she know all this about Dad."

I suppressed my thoughts of that woman's reputation of supposedly being right so many times and instead wholeheartedly agreed with Mom's last remark. Anything to get her out of her wretched mood. Apparently, I had hit the right nerve. In later years, every time she talked about this affair, she remarked on my words, saying that it was this conclusion from her nine year old child that had snapped her out of her depression. I never could see anything remarkable in what I had said to comfort her. But then, who can predict how damaging, or as in this case, reassuring a small and insignificant remark could turn out.

Finally, one afternoon of early September 1945, we got word that my Dad was alive and ready to be released from a P.O.W. camp in Freising, just north of Munich. A former German soldier, already released from there, had stopped by our place to deliver this message. The many questions my mother had about Dad's condition, however, he couldn't or wouldn't answer. One burning question in particular worried Mom.

"Was my husband wounded?" she repeated many times, but all the man would say was, "Look, Ma'am, I don't know your husband. He didn't look wounded. I only had a brief glimpse of him as I was leaving. He had heard that I was heading for Starnberg and through the fence he hollered this message for you and how to find you."

Mother fixed a hot meal for the man and gave him some American cigarettes that I had collected for bartering. We never saw him again.

Mom immediately inquired about the possibility to travel to Freising to see Dad, but there was no longer a direct way to get there. She decided to take the train to Munich the next day and see how she could continue on to Freising from there. Early the next morning, Mom prepared to leave. She said she would visit my grandparents first and then see how to proceed from there. Not knowing what to expect, she decided I should stay behind. She knew I was pretty self-sufficient, and I counted on that our American friend, Mr. Sonn, wouldn't let me starve.

That very evening she was back and Dad was with her. While Mom had still been at Grandpa's place, trying to figure out how to get to Freising, Dad had showed up there as well. He had been released and had hitched a ride to Munich. Before going on to Starnberg, he wanted to stop by at my grandparents first. And now he was back.

I was shocked by the way Dad looked. His black hair had all turned to gray, his skin was tanned as never before and instead of his glasses with the handsome frame he wore some wire-rimmed, round granny glasses. He seemed to be just skin and bones and still, the old uniform that he had been given to wear was two sizes too small. But we were so glad to have him back in one piece.

But Dad really wasn't in one piece, so to speak. Even though there were no obvious signs like a missing arm or leg, he still had been severely wounded. After Mom had made him comfortable and he had a bath and something to eat, Dad started relating his ordeal to us. And these were his very words:

"After being transferred to northern Italy in January of 1944, I was assigned to administrative duty, with some Italian civilians working for me. As the war was drawing to its end in that region, the situation became terribly confused by the questionable loyalties of the Italians. As the American troops were advancing from the south, whole sections of the Italian military, up to then allies of Germany, had quickly switched sides and joined the American onslaught. Many other units simply disappeared into the woods. The civilians working for me, however, kept showing up faithfully for duty every day without fail.

Also, there were Italian guerrillas fighting against their former allies, the Germans. There were three categories of guerrillas, distinguishable by the different colors of their bandannas. There were the Monarchist, the Republicans, and then there were the ones that wore red — the Communists. They were the fiercest.

Early in April 1945, the fighting approached the area where I was stationed. One afternoon, heavy gun fire could be heard echoing from the south. All telephone lines were dead, effectively cutting off our outpost from the rest of the world. Our building was at the bottom of a circular depression surrounded by mountains. The next morning, the civilians failed to show up for work and no more traffic was seen on the only road leading down to us. No more supplies could be expected. We were on our own.

The following night, our building was attacked. The big guns we had been hearing in the distance, until two days ago were now mysteriously silent, but machine gun fire came down from all of the surrounding hills. As the enemy started to advance down the slopes, we returned the fire, driving the attackers far enough back to be out of range. There were about thirty men with me in our building when it all started. Being highest in rank, I was in command.

The shooting went on all night. We had only three machine guns, one carbine per man and I, being an officer, had a side-arm. But, we had plenty of ammunition. By morning, we could tell that the attackers were Italian guerrillas. It soon developed into a standoff, with both sides holding their ground. Where there had been about three hundred guerrillas at first, there were now roughly twice as many. As they had no canons or other heavy artillery and could not come close enough to throw grenades, their only hope lay in their ever increasing numbers. But my soldiers and I fired out of every button hole, effectively keeping them at bay, incidentally inflicting heavy enemy casualties. This went on for two days and nights. A few of my men were shot by sniper commandos that had sneaked up unnoticed, but we always managed to drive them back, killing a fair number of them in the process.

On the third morning, one of my men called me to an upstairs window out of which he had been watching the road. He had spotted a priest walking down towards our building, waving a large white flag. I told my men not to shoot, but to keep a sharp eye on the surrounding hills. Just inside the main door, I awaited the arrival of the man in the black cloth. I beckoned him inside and he entered willingly. He was an elderly man with a friendly face and sad blue eyes. In spite of the morning's chill, he wiped the perspiration from his forehead and gratefully accepted the chair I offered him. He sat down and silently looked around at our battered walls and glassless windows. Then he broke his silence. He asked if I was the man in charge here. I nodded, surprised at his flawless German. He then asked me why we were still fighting.

'The war is over,' he said, 'it has been over for thirty-six hours now and you are still shooting and inflicting heavy casualties.'

We had known that the end had to be near, but that it was already over came as a great surprise. We had been completely cut off and we simply didn't know. He patiently explained the details of the surrender of the German forces in all of northern Italy that had taken place two days ago. I believed the man, he seemed too sincere to be deceiving us. I told him that, of course, in view of this we would surrender immediately and asked him to explain our situation to his people. He promised he would and gave me the white flag he had carried. While the priest was walking back to his people, I informed my soldiers of the developments and ordered one of them to fasten the white flag to our front door. There were only twelve of us left, the others had been killed during the past twenty-four hours.

The twelve of us carried our weapons outside and placed them in plain view against the wall. Then we waited for them to come and take us prisoners. It didn't take long. Six heavily armed guerrillas adorned with red bandannas came jogging towards us. Communists! The priest was not with them. The hate in their eyes was plain to see. One of them, apparently their leader, motioned us all back into our large front room. I knew enough Italian to understand when he hollered who our commanding officer was. I stepped forward, expecting surrender formalities. Instead I got a fist in my face that sent my glasses flying, and me sprawling across the reception desk behind me. Six machine guns, trained point blank at me, prevented any retaliation on my part. Raising myself, I felt blood trickling down my chin and into my collar. Then he screamed at us to line up against the back wall of the room. He looked at us for a moment, and then, with his five comrades watching, he raised his machine gun and opened fire at all of us. I felt like I had been clubbed across my stomach and went down with all the others, but I *was not dead. Aware of the acrid smell of burnt gun powder and in agonizing pain, I tried to raise myself up along the wall. I saw another one of my men also stumbling back to his feet, the others were lying in a pile where they had been mowed down. As the guerrillas turned to leave, however, their leader became aware that two of us were still not dead. He fired another round, hitting the other soldier squarely in the forehead. Then he turned towards me. I saw the fire exploding from his gun and felt another kick against my midsection. We both collapsed and stayed down.*

How long I had lain there unconscious, I could not tell. The next thing I remember was someone manipulating my hands. It quickly became clear to me that I was being stripped of the rings on my finger. I pulled my hand back and moaned in pain. My consciousness returned full force and with it I became aware of a terrible pain in my vitals. Outside, darkness was settling. Then I recognized the people that were bent over me. They were two of the Italian civilians, Arturo and Marina Rosselini, a married couple that had been working for me. Now they had returned to strip the dead of their belongings. When they realized that I was still alive, they both broke out in tears and lamented my condition with profound compassion.

'Lieutenant,' they sobbed, 'don't worry, we will help you. We'll get you to a hospital and you'll be all right again soon.'

I had always gotten along fine with those people and apparently they had liked me as well. Together they dragged me out to their little Fiat Topolino, a pint-sized two-seater, and stowed me into that tiny space behind the front seats. My pains were excruciating. I kept drifting in and out of consciousness during the bumpy ride to the nearest hospital. Once they arrived at the hospital, they again carried me and brought me inside to the reception desk. As soon as these people recognized me as being German they shouted, 'A German! Get him out of here, we don't want him.' No matter how my rescuers pleaded, they were sent on in search of another hospital. Arturo and Marina put me back behind the seats. I passed out again.

This was repeated at every hospital they tried. Finally, they came to a hospital that was run by Catholic nuns. It was the seventh medical center they had approached, but here they felt I would certainly be admitted. But not even there was I welcome.

'We don't want any Germans,' the nun at the front desk insisted. Arturo was furious.

'You are Catholics, this soldier is also a Catholic and so are we,' he screamed. 'I wish to talk to your Mother Superior, and pronto,' he demanded.

When the nun in charge finally arrived, she only repeated what the others had already stated, 'No Germans!' I heard Arturo say, 'And you call yourself a bride of God? Shame on you, Sister.'

The contempt in his voice was undeniable.

'All right then, bring him in,' she finally consented. As they carried me in, no one raised a hand to help them nor did they bother to offer a stretcher. They ushered us into a room full of beds, most of them were occupied. Bypassing several empty beds they pointed to a cot in the far corner and had *them lay me down on that. Drifting in and out, I was barely aware of their tearful good-byes. I did hear them promise to come and visit me, but I never saw them again as long as I was in that hospital. Later I found out that they had come several times, but each time they had been turned away at the front door and were not allowed to see me.*

Now I was alone, in a room full of people. Whenever I was conscious I waited for someone to look after my injuries, but no one came. I had become aware of three wounds, all of them in my midsection. Still wearing not only my uniform but several layers of other clothing, I was unable to determine the extent of my injuries. We had known that sooner or later we would have to give up the building and run, so everyone wore every piece of clothing he owned, so as not to be encumbered when forced to travel. Now blood kept oozing through the cloth at all three wounds. Especially my back felt warm and wet.

The pain was excruciating. I started to call out to attract attention, but all I got in response was curses from the other patients. I drifted off again. When I came to, all the others were eating. On an ammunition box beside my bed stood a plate with food. I had no appetite, all I felt was the intense pain.

Near my cot, I noticed a wire hanging down with a switch-button on its end. Struggling to reach for it, I finally caught it and pressed the button. A nun appeared, wanting to know who had called. When she found out it had been I, she turned around and wanted to leave. This time I really screamed, imploring her to come back. Grudgingly she approached and barked at me, 'What do you want?'

'A doctor,' I moaned, 'and something for my pain.'

She told me there was no doctor, until the next morning and without a doctor she could not give me anything. I told her to at least give me some morphine to stop the pain. During the war, I had seen enough instances where morphine was given to the wounded, at least until something could be done for them. At first, she refused, but finally, after a long period of arguing, she said she would come back with a shot for me. She did come back with a syringe. When I asked her if it was morphine, she just nodded her head and administered the shot. I asked her to clean me up, but she absolutely refused and stomped out of the room. That shot did not help at all. The pain was as bad as before. Often I blacked out and I became grateful for these periods of relief.

The next morning, a doctor made his rounds. When he came to the room I was in, he went from bed to bed, talking to all the patients. He completely ignored me and prepared to leave. I hollered for him, but he kept on going, slamming the door behind him. I began to feel desperate. How long was this supposed to go on, I wondered. My mattress was soaked with blood from the wound in my back. I was still wearing all these clothes and I started to smell. The next time I came to, I started to unbutton my uniform jacket. In spite of my extreme pain I somehow managed to rid myself of some of my garments. Everything was soaked with blood and puss. I had to fight nausea from the horrible stench. Then the nun appeared. One of the patients waved at her and whispered something to her. She looked over at me and then she left the room. Shortly, she was back with towels and water. She came to my bed, helped me get out of my sweater and T-shirt, that had resisted my earlier attempts and proceeded to clean me up a little. When she saw that the mess had gone clear through the mattress, the cot and on to the floor, she brought in a clean cot and helped me get onto that. She never said a word. This time when I asked for morphine, she didn't argue and just nodded her head. She returned and gave me a shot, but again there was no relief from it.

I had drifted off again. Now there was food and water near my cot. I wasn't hungry, but I greedily drank the water. The pain was as bad as ever, but no doctor came to see me. Last time I hollered at the doctor while he checked the other patients, he turned around, yelling, 'I can't treat you, someone else will come for you.' 'Yes, he's probably talking about an undertaker,' I thought.

And so it went on. I felt weaker and weaker with each passing day. The pain had not let up at all. I had become delirious. No one came to clean me up anymore and the shots they gave me had no effect. I suspected they were injecting me with water instead of morphine. I saw no more hope and in my delirium I just wished to quickly end it all. I was practically floating in blood and puss and the smell, once again, was unbearable. I waited for darkness and hoped that all the other patients would be asleep. In spite of the horrible pain, I raised myself up and, holding on to the wall, I managed to stand on my feet for the first time. I reached for the bell cable, pulled it tight and wrapped it about my neck. I wanted to jump off the cot and strangle myself. One brief moment of hesitation was quickly abolished as I looked down at my cot. By the shine of the feeble night light I saw the bloody, stinking mess that I had been forced to lay in all those days. I wasn't exactly able to jump but instead just let myself fall off the cot. My body hit the floor while the entire cable ripped off the wall and fell in a heap all around me. Someone summoned the nurse and now I was really in trouble. I ignored her hysteric screams and tried to get back onto my filthy cot. Cruelly I was hoisted onto the cot where, by a stroke of luck, I passed out into oblivion.

The next morning, Mother Superior came and chewed me out using language I never thought a nun would know of, much less repeat. I desperately tried to stay alert enough to talk to her. After she ran out of wind, I told her that since they refused to treat me here, in God's name take me out of my misery. I told her to go and find some Communist to shoot me and finish the job. Now she really raged, admonishing me about taking God's name in vain. I turned away from her and she stomped out of the room.

That afternoon, I heard a commotion coming from the hallway. Then suddenly, the door was jerked open and an armed guerrilla stormed in. It was a Communist, as was evident by the red bandanna he wore. He was clutching a machine gun and gruffly asked who it was that wanted to be shot. Everyone pointed at me, while I was struggling to a sitting position. He looked at me with a grim, but doubting expression. I pulled back my sheets, bared my chest and nodded. He pointed his machine gun at me and for a long time he just stared at me. All the other patients had turned away, some had hidden under their blankets. Then, without saying a word, he abruptly turned around and marched out the door.

I felt shattered. There would be no relief from that awful pain. I just knew that I would die slowly and in unspeakable agony. From then on, I noticed that the other patients had stopped ignoring me. Some even talked to me, as much as our different languages allowed. A few of them would even see to it that my water glass stayed filled. For that they would take the food I never touched, but they were welcome to it; I felt food was the last thing I needed. However, they could do little else. Unable to move, I was forced to stay and rot away in my own filth. The fibers of all the many layers of clothing I had been wearing had all been driven into my body ahead of the bullets. By now they were festering out of my wounds with a steady flow of puss.

I never was a very religious man, but one day I asked for a priest. None ever came. I had hoped that if a priest sees the sorry conditions I had to put up with, that perhaps he could effect a change for the better. I was out of luck once more.

Several more days had gone by since the guerilla's refusal to shoot me. I marvelled at the fact that I was still alive. I surmised that it had to be my prior excellent physical condition that allowed me to hang on for so long. I had been the proud recipient of the "German Athletic Medal" in gold. However, by now I was so weak, that when I heard another commotion outside, I was barely able to turn my head, to see who was coming through the door. To my great surprise, I saw soldiers in combat uniforms with netted helmets talking to the head nun. They were Americans. One of them I recognized to be a Captain, by the bars on his uniform. He did all the talking.

They briefly went from bed to bed and then they stopped at my little cot. My filthy uniform jacket was still laying where I had dropped it a long time ago. By it they realized that I was a German officer. The others had all been Italian civilians and had received good care and treatment. The captain raised my stained sheet and saw and smelled the filth. He turned to the head nun and asked a few questions. Then he started yelling at her.

I understood enough to know that he was chewing her out for her deplorable attitude towards me. She cursed him and stomped out. After he had calmed down some, the captain started talking to me in German. He told me that he would send for an ambulance to take me to an American military hospital and that I had nothing to worry about. He lit a cigarette and handed it to me. I was so weak I could barely raise my hand to take it. He then ordered one of his men to stay with me and accompany me to their facilities, while he had to attend to other duties. The soldier could not speak German, but he kept smiling and kept encouraging me with his body language. He offered me a candy bar, which I had to refuse. I still felt that food was the last thing I needed. So, he kept me supplied with water and he also lit up cigarettes for me.

I must have passed out again, but I came to when I felt myself being lifted off my cot. Soldiers laid me on a stretcher and carried me out. I heard the other patients calling out to say good-bye; they wished me well. I was too delirious to respond, but I did notice that even the stretcher felt more comfortable than that primitive cot. Again I passed out.

The next thing I remember was being in a brightly lit room, with two medics, working to clean me up. Everyone was friendly and manipulated me with the utmost care. I was so happy, I could have cried. As soon as I was cleaned up, two doctors in uniform gave me a thorough examination. One of them spoke German perfectly. He told me that I had been shot in the gut from the front and that the projectile had exited at my lower back. This wound was the largest. Another shot had also grazed my right side, just above the hip bone. As far as he could see, either no serious damage had been done to any vital organs or the damage had already healed to a point where an operation at this time would not be prudent. The fact that I had not eaten anything solid also was a blessing, according to him. The doctors had heard about the miserable treatment I had to suffer by those Italian nuns. To them, it was utterly unthinkable to treat anyone like this, enemy or not. In Germany, many hospitals were also staffed by nuns. On occasions some of them were known to act a little grumpy. But behavior like this from any nun, anywhere in the world, simply could never have been imagined.

The doctor, who spoke German, told me that he was prescribing something to ease my pain and that, at least for awhile, I would be fed intravenously. It would be a sugar solution, to sustain me until I would be in shape to eat solid food again.

'As soon as your wounds have healed,' he said, 'and as soon as we get some strength back into you, I will put you on the accelerated P.O.W. release list.

You'll be with your loved ones as quickly as possible.'

I thanked the doctor for everything. The prescribed pain medication worked wonders. As soon as my pain started to abate, I felt like I was in heaven. For the first time, since I had been shot, I drifted off into a contented slumber.

Every day the doctors examined me, and day by day I felt some of my strength returning. They kept me relatively free of pain and with their professional care the puss flow of my wounds gradually subsided. My eyes were examined and I was given a pair of glasses. Now, at least, I could see properly again. Weeks went by and I seemed to have no adverse after-effects. I had been eating solid food for quite a while, felt clean, and couldn't wait to be sent home.

One morning, I was asked to see the commanding officer. When I arrived at his office, he cordially greeted me and invited me to sit down across the desk from him. I had seen him several times on my walks through the installation, but had never met him. He tossed a pack of cigarettes across the desk and as I took one he told me to keep the pack. In very passable German, he told me that he had heard about the abominable treatment I had received in that Italian hospital. He asked me what I thought about all that now. I told him that all I wanted to do was to get home to my family and try to forget this whole sordid mess, as quickly as possible.

For a long while he looked at me, then he said, 'I must congratulate you on your wise attitude and especially on your miraculous recovery. We are going to release you and put you onto the next transport going north.' In spite of the most urgent hopes I had

had about my going home soon, I could hardly believe what I heard. I would finally be back with my family. But then, I didn't even know if they had survived the bombs at home. Horrible reports had been filtering through, about the severity of the bombing of German cities, of the many firestorms caused by saturation bombings of residential areas, where civilians by the thousands, mostly women and children, burned to death each night, and of the appalling misery of the homeless survivors. Before I had been transferred to Italy, we had lost everything we had ever owned in Munich. My business and our apartment had been lost to the bombs. But that had been nothing compared to the ferocity of the enemy's air raids during the last few months of the war. I fervently hoped that at least the little town of Starnberg had been spared by the bombs.

I thanked the officer for everything and told him how much I respected the Americans for their humane and civilized conduct and for everything they had done for me. He told me that the doctor would see me now, with further instructions and a supply of medication. He came around his desk and accompanied me to the door. He wished me well; his handshake was firm and genuine.

That afternoon, the doctor came and performed a thorough inspection of my healed wounds. He told me to see our family doctor as soon as I arrived at home. Handing me a generous supply of antibiotics and some tablets to relieve the pain, he told me to be ready at 6:00 a.m., the next day.

The sun wasn't up yet, when I, along with about a dozen other P.O.W.s, showed up at the motor pool's parking lot. A large GMC truck, with the engine running, was parked off to one side. There were two soldiers in the cab and another one in the back. This one motioned us to come aboard. I was the last one to climb up and over the lowered tailgate. That's when it happened. I never did find out how or why. Either I had slipped and lost my footing or perhaps the driver had jerked the heavy truck into motion, but before I realized it, I had fallen off the truck. I hit the ground and sprawled on the pavement. By my fall, the cooking utensils fastened to my belt, were driven into my side with such force that it knocked the wind out of me. The pain was severe and I was unable to get up. A stretcher was brought for me, while the truck with my more fortunate comrades proceeded out of the gate on its journey north. I had been left behind. Of course, I realized that I was in no shape to travel just now, but the thought of not going home hurt deeply, nevertheless.

The doctor couldn't believe it when he saw me again back at the hospital. He examined me and, suspicious of a possible broken rib, ordered to have me x-rayed. Later that day, he returned with my x-ray pictures and a very serious expression on his face.

'You didn't break any ribs,' he said, 'You received some severe and painful bruises, but nothing significant. You should be ready to travel in a couple of weeks.'

Then he gave me a long and searching look. I began to feel uncomfortable especially by his still serious expression. 'Well, that's good news,' I said, 'but what seems to be the problem?' I asked.

Without a word, he handed me my x-rays. I held them to the light and saw parts of a spine, the lower

115

curve of ribs and something else. Something that should not have been there, something that just didn't belong there.

Right in front of my spine was a solid object about the size of the last digit of my thumb. This was the side view of my body. I reached for the other x-ray, which was taken from the front. There again, about one millimeter to the side of my spine, was this solid object. I looked at the doctor. He had been watching me. Now he said, 'That, my friend, is a twelve millimeter bullet from a machine gun. Your third wound, the one on your side, apparently was not made by a grazing bullet, as we had so far assumed, but instead was caused by a direct hit. The bullet stopped one millimeter before it splintered your spine. Had it gone on just that much further, you would have been dead or at least paralyzed.

'You are extremely lucky. It seems a miracle that you are alive and relatively well,' the doctor continued, 'I would say a one-in-a-million chance.'

I was stunned. 'What are my chances, Doctor?' I asked. He told me I would be examined more thoroughly and that he would seek the opinion of some of his colleagues, some of them internists. He would keep me informed on their findings. For the time being, I was confined to my bed once again.

The next morning the doctor was back.

'Here is how we see it,' he said, 'We could operate and remove the bullet. The chances of survival, however, would be fifty-fifty, at best. It is, therefore, our recommendation to leave it alone, for now. Sometimes foreign objects like this,' he explained, 'start to wander through the body. If that happens,

it could either drift to a more accessible location where it could then be removed with little danger. Or it may drift farther against the spine or into vital organs where it could cause paralysis or even death.' He advised me to consult my doctor in Germany and have semi-annual x-rays taken to keep track of the thing.

This was a new trauma I had to deal with. Since I was unable to do anything about the situation, I decided not to let useless worrying slow my healing process. Within a couple of weeks, my bruises indeed had healed to the point that I was once again ready for travel. Word about my condition had gotten around and a number of American physicians and even some Italian doctors visited me during these two weeks. They studied my x-rays and they all told me how fortunate I had been. Then came the day when I was finally able to travel home.

This time, I was extra careful to avoid any further mishaps. The ride on the big GMC truck was uncomfortable, but I thought that with every turn of the wheels I was getting closer to home. The first night, we bivouacked on a mountain pass in Switzerland. The next morning, we were transferred onto a train. American soldiers accompanied us, acting as our guards. The journey had taken us first through the Italian, then the Swiss, and later, on through the German Alps. The breathtaking panoramas were unforgettably beautiful.

The trip proceeded uneventfully, always north, steadily homewards. Then I suddenly realized that we would be passing near our weekend house in Starnberg. In the crowded boxcar, I wormed myself towards the open door so I could look out. Sure

117

enough, we were traveling along the tracks that bordered our property. As we got close, I strained to look through the dense foliage and at one time I even got a quick glimpse of our house. It was still standing! It really hurt not to be able to stop and I felt like jumping out. Just in time, I told myself to be patient. I had had too many setbacks already and didn't need to bring on another one.

While passing through what was left of Munich, the extent of the devastation took my breath away. It was far worse than I had imagined in my most fatalistic speculations. In Freising, we were assigned bunks in some barracks, but in view of my wounds, I was admitted to the hospital tent where I received preferred treatment and extra rations. It would still take several days to be processed, as we soon found out. I heard of a man being released to Starnberg. He was already outside the fence when I hollered at him to please notify my family. He took the address and promised he would go there. Then he was gone.

Two days later, I was finally released. A ride to Munich was arranged and then I was on my own. Not knowing how to get to Starnberg the fastest, I decided to first look up Grandpa and Grandma to get some news about my family. They lived within walking distance and I could only hope that their home was still intact. Looking at all the ruins surrounding me, it seemed a miracle that the house in which they had lived was still standing. It had received damage, especially to the roof and to the uppermost apartments, but the second floor, where they resided, seemed to be untouched. I walked up and rang the bell. You can't imagine my surprise to meet Mother there."

We were deeply moved by Dad's account. My mind went over what we had just heard. He had received two gut shots two days after the war was over in northern Italy. He had not expected to survive his injuries. But, thanks to the benevolent American soldiers, he had survived. Suddenly, a startling realization came to me, when my mind reflected on the words of old Mrs. Dölken, the astrologer. It was a sobering recollection and I began to feel quite ashamed for my quick and immature judgement of the old woman.

That evening, I looked for Mr. Sonn to tell him about my Dad's return and invited him to come and meet Dad. He came as soon as he could get away. Mr. Sonn brought a carton of cigarettes and some candy bars as a gift to celebrate Dad's return. The two men got along famously. They had something in common: They were both soldiers and neither one ever had had any use for the war. Dad had to tell his story again. We all agreed that it truly was a miracle that Dad was still alive.

Mr. Sonn asked Dad about his opinion of the American P.O.W. camp in Freising. Dad had nothing but praise. That particular camp had been run very efficiently and the German soldiers had been treated decently and with respect.

The author (center) with his Dad and
Mr. Sonn — September 1945.

Then came the time when Mr. Sonn had to leave. It was a sunny morning that day in late September of 1945. He came to say "Good-bye." When he walked away, I accompanied him to a treeless lot further down on our street that had been used by the troops to park their vehicles and equipment. A number of small trucks were assembled and the soldiers, carrying their duffel bags climbed up and sat down on the benches. Another solemn handshake and he had to jump aboard as well. I watched as the truck started to roll out onto the street. I waved to him, but I felt sad and so helpless. There was nothing I could do to keep him here, I didn't want him to leave. It broke my heart seeing him wave for the last time as the truck disappeared in the distance, knowing I would never see him again. Voluntarily, I went to bed early that night to nurse my grief. I had lost another dear and true friend. The many good times we had shared together passed in succession before my mind. Then I recalled Mr. Sonn's departure. As I once again saw him being driven off in that small truck, I cried like a baby. For days, I felt downhearted, subdued, depressed and restless. He did write a letter once to let us know he had made it home all right. It came from Passaic, New Jersey. We wrote back, but that was the end of it.

I knew that it would take me awhile to get used to Dad being home all day. In my early childhood I had only seen him on weekends for little intervals. During the week he had been at his store and by the time he came home I was usually already in bed. Then, since he went to war, I had seen him only during his short leaves from the air force. Now I was eagerly looking forward to this new experience.

*

Other soldiers had moved in. We became acquainted with quite a few of them. There weren't nearly as many as before and several other neighboring houses had been given back to their owners. On October 10, 1945, General Dwight D. Eisenhower had lifted the anti-fraternizing directive for the U.S. troops, making the interactions between the GIs and the German population a lot more amiable.

There was a large mansion on the property to the north of our fence. This one, the military retained and used it as their headquarters. Every morning at five thirty, they fired a canon across the lake. Then, while playing their National Anthem over a powerful public address system, they would raise their flag up a tall pole. At the same time every evening, another canon shot was fired and while the anthem was played the flag was taken in. When I heard that morning-shot for the first time, I jumped out of bed looking for cover.

Ripped out of deep sleep, I thought bombs were falling again. It took me a while to realize that the war had been over. The next morning I heard it again, raised one eyelid and, knowing what it was, kept on sleeping. From then on I never even woke up from it.

All during the day, an American radio station, A.F.N. Munich, could be heard broadcasting news, commercials and music across the countryside. The music was coming out of an enormous speaker that the soldiers had mounted atop a tall post which they had planted in the far corner of our property. Much to the chagrin of the adult population, but the children enjoyed it. My favorite program came weekdays from three o'clock to three thirty and was called "Hillbilly Guesthouse". I sat myself right under that speaker and, leaning against the post, I enjoyed songs from Eddy Arnold, Tex Ritter, Hank Snow, Hank Williams and many other country singers. I learned these songs by heart and would sing them all day long. Only, I didn't know what the words meant. I couldn't speak English then.

Chapter Nine

War Games

I have mentioned the Volkssturm earlier, but allow me to reiterate in a bit more detail: By autumn of 1944 all the young and able German men had been drafted to fight at the different fronts. This had left the interior of the homeland essentially vulnerable and defenseless. When it had become obvious that the war was starting towards a bad ending for Germany, Nazi officials had dictated the creation of the Volkssturm. This was to be an organization of elderly men and all the women and children. They had been ordered, in case of an enemy invasion, to defend the Fatherland *to the last drop of blood.* It had been organized similar to the Air-raid Blockwart system, where in each city-block a Block Captain was responsible to recruit a number of people for rescue and clean-up duties after bomb raids, to make sure the black-out laws were strictly adhered to and to guide the population to the nearest bomb shelter.

In order to accomplish the Volkssturm's intended purpose successfully, the population would have to be armed. This did not take long. No matter how small a village or hamlet, each suddenly had at least one Volkssturm block captain. At strategic locations, in the forest as well as in open fields and pastures, caches of weapons and ammunition had been buried in sealed crates, to be dug up and used by the people of the Volkssturm whenever the need would arise. Each such operation had been supervised by the local Volkssturm commander, while Russian POWs had volunteered their labor in exchange for preferred treatment at the camps.

The various Volkssturm officials had held organized, public meetings to educate the population in the handling of these weapons. Attendances at such meetings had been surprisingly poor. Unlike the air raid Block Captain system, which had proved beneficial and had made sense, the Volkssturm had been perceived as a pointless and hare-brained idea by most. Open rebellion, however, had been out of the question. A report of such an incident by the Volkssturm official would have resulted in the immediate arrest of the rebels and quite possibly in their ultimate transfer to one of the dreaded concentration camps.

It remains a little known fact to the rest of the world just how much the German people were afraid to end up in one of these camps. While little was known what exactly went on in there, a transfer to a KZ, as they were called, was generally considered a one-way ticket to doom. Not only Jews perished in these camps, as the world was and still is led to believe. The fact is that any German citizen daring to openly speak out against Hitler or the Nazi regime would end up in a KZ to share the same fate.

There was another aspect to these camps, however. A lot of criminals, convicted of murder, rape or any other capital or violent crime ended up in these camps and were worked mercilessly on projects for the public's benefit.

This particular aspect of these camps, however, was considered right and proper by the majority of the population, since it kept hardened criminals off the streets, presented no burden to the taxpayers and served as a powerful and most effective deterrent for would-be criminals. It was well known that rapists, for instance, were immediately altered to assure that they could never rape again. On the other hand, any KZ inmate could trade for preferred treatment by volunteering for scientific experiments and thereby benefit mankind. What was happening to political prisoners, however, was not known and therefore feared the most.

When the time had finally arrived for the Volkssturm's efforts to be put into operation, there had been no more organization or leadership whatsoever. By that time, the various Volkssturm captains, most of them being avid Nazi sympathizers, had all disappeared into hiding. I know of not one example where any of these weapons were ever used for their intended purpose. At least in our area everyone had been glad that the war would be over soon and that no more bombs would be raining down on us. No one had any desire to fulfill the Volkssturm's goal to delay the end and prolong the agony. Especially in view of the futility of such a scheme the population had rather welcomed the invaders with open arms and, at least in our area, not one shot had been fired by any civilian.

*

Several of the children had secretly watched the burial of such a weapon cache in a forest near my home. Now the war was over, but we still had no toys. Because of this, a number of us got together to dig up that stuff and play with it. I was ten years old at the time and most of our group was of the same age. Only a couple of boys were fourteen and fifteen. It didn't take us long to find the crates, but because of their weight, we were unable to lift them out of the ground. We therefore pried the lids off and emptied the contents onto the forest floor.

Everything was securely wrapped in heavily waxed tarpaulins and then again in waxed paper. There were carbines with bayonets, machine guns complete with tripods, large and small hand grenades, appropriate ammunition and complete and detailed instructions for the assembly and use of the different items. We deemed the grenades as too dangerous and returned them to the bottom of the empty crates. The rest however, was promptly assembled as per instruction and under the supervision of the older boys.

Then it was time to try shooting the rifles for the first time. These were regular 8 mm infantry carbines with Mauser locks. Their large size and bulky weight, however, made them quite awkward for us. We also objected to the tremendous kick of these weapons and soon laid them down in favor of other things. There were also small caliber rifles. Most of them were 6 mm Floberts, also with Mauser locks and very easy for us to operate. We preferred these for their light or non-existing recoil. After firing many rounds, most of us became quite proficient in their use. In war-time Germany, toys were practically non-existent and we were used to play with anything at all and to use our imagination. Now, we felt we had found the ideal "toys".

Soon, we staged regular "War-Games". First we shot at tree trunks that we saw as enemy soldiers, but soon they became too easy to hit. This also became boring because these shot resulted in no reaction, no motion. Much better targets were overhead branches, representing the dreaded B-17 bombers. We fired at them until they would fall to the ground and then zeroed in on the next one. As we became even more proficient, we started shooting pine cones, which had become fighter planes, off of the highest tree limbs.

We happily watched as these pine cones came down or disintegrated when hit, and we were delighted, now at least something happened, something moved. For each hit we were rewarded with the Iron Cross. These decorations were fashioned from used wooden matches tied together with string. Most of us had not had that much fun for as long as we could remember.

We did not worry about being discovered even in spite of the racket we made. For a time after the German surrender, there was practically no law enforcement in existence. The German police had been temporarily replaced by the US Military Police. The MPs, as we soon discovered, would not venture into the forest upon hearing gunfire, so we were relatively safe from detection and frankly, we had a ball.

When it was time to go home we covered everything with the tarpaulins and hid the whole treasure under shot-off branches. We vowed to keep quiet about the whole thing and not to take anything home with us. (In spite of this, several of us did sneak out in the dark of night, when our mothers thought us sound asleep, and "secured" one or two of these Flobert rifles, along with plenty ammunition for our personal use.)

Since there was no school at the time, we were able to continue our new-found hobby the next day without delay. This time we started to assemble one of the machine guns. Under the supervision of the older boys and with the help of the written instructions, we soon had one of them ready and were working on the tripod. It took several of us to lift that heavy gun onto its stand, but we did it. An ammunition belt was clipped into position and we were ready. The trunk of a dead pine tree became the target. We put the selector to "single" and each had a turn at firing at the target. Then we moved the selector to the "rapid" position. The oldest of us aimed at the target and pulled the trigger. What came next happened so fast that it caught all of us off guard. The front of the tripod raised up and the whole thing toppled backwards to the ground, spraying bullets every which way. Debris, branches, pine cones and what-not rained down on us. The noise was horrendous. Puffs of dust appeared wherever bullets hit the ground. The rat-tat-tat of the heavy gun would not quit until the entire belt had run through.

We were stunned. At the time we did not realize how lucky we had been that no one was hurt. For a long while we couldn't figure out what had happened and the younger boys quickly lost interest in the machine guns. The teenagers finally came up with an explanation: Because of the combined recoil of all these many bullets, the gun had kicked up straight into the air and had taken the entire tripod with it. If we had only read on a little farther, the instructions would have told us what these funny-looking corkscrews were that we had found together with clips and turnbuckles. These should have been screwed into the ground and secured to the two forward legs of the tripod. This would have held the gun in position. However, why the entire belt had fed through, before it stopped firing, remained a mystery.

By the time I got back there the next day, the older boys had been busy. They insisted on having another go at the machine gun. The rest of us were not interested and had fun shooting pine cones. After awhile we noticed that the machine gun had again been made ready. A new belt was in place and the legs were properly secured. The target was still the old dead pine's trunk. All was set, but for some reason the two boys hesitated. Then it came: They thought it necessary for two of us youngsters to help hold down the front legs of the tripod. They had a hard time trying to convince us that they desperately needed our help. Finally I and one other boy volunteered for the job.

Each of us laid flat on the ground near a front leg. We had to reach up and hold down the tripod leg with all our little weight. Before we knew it, the gun rattled off and this time there were no problems. The spray of bullets hit the target. The wood of the trunk splintered until the old tree came crashing down. We could actually feel it through the ground as it hit in a cloud of dust. But again the gun had kept firing until the entire belt was through.

This accomplished, we no longer had any desire to play with that machine gun. It was just too much effort and made entirely too much noise. We all helped together and dragged it to a nearby ravine, gave it a push and watched as it tumbled down.

Another crate contained more grenades and also spools of fuses. Some were marked "slow" but most were identified as "fast." We took all the fuses. The older boys proposed to show us how to build bombs to blow up stumps. For want of proper toys, we had all been pretty proficient in making harmless key-bombs. All that was needed was a hollow door-key, a blunted nail that fit into the hollow of the key, a piece of string and some matches. The string was used to loosely tie the key and the nail-head together. Sulphur from the matches was scraped off and inserted into the hollow of the key. The blunt end of the nail then followed the sulphur into the key. The whole contraption could be unobtrusively held by the string in one hand and when the nail-head was banged against a hard surface, the suddenly compressed sulphur exploded. It sounded like firecrackers when they went off, and we had used them to startle unsuspecting adults. This, however, promised to be something quite different.

We were told to go to the dump and bring back as many old tin-cans as we could find. Preferably cans with the lid still hanging on them. At home, after doing our various chores for our mothers, we didn't have too much trouble getting away. If asked what we were up to, we always answered, "Oh we're out in the woods, playing." As far as we were concerned we had told the truth.

We showed up with quite a few empty cans the next day. One of the older boys, his name was Fritz, was carrying a belt of anti-aircraft ammunition and set it down on the ground in front of us. Then he brought a rock and several smaller stones. Fritz squatted down and with a bayonet pried one of the cartridges from the belt. He placed it on the rock and showed us how the bullet could be pulled out. He used a stone for a hammer and the rock as an anvil and loosened the crimp of the cartridge by tapping on it all around until the bullet fell out. Then he dumped the dark-grey powder from inside the cartridge into one of the tin-cans that we had brought along. He told us to continue with that until the can would be almost full.

It was a slow and tedious process. We had to remove the powder from many cartridges before the first small can was ready. Under the supervision of Helmut, the other teenager, some of us kept working to fill a second can, while Fritz led the rest of us to a large ancient stump.

Again, using the bayonet, he started digging a small tunnel that led directly under the stump, which for us had become an enemy bunker. We took over with the digging until Fritz was satisfied that it was deep enough. He then produced a spool of fuse and stuck the end of it deep down into the powder inside the can. He bent the lid down and closed it as good as well as possible. The can was then placed under the stump and the hole filled in with stones and loose dirt. Fritz played out a long length of fuse and led it behind a large fir tree about sixty feet from the stump. Everyone was alerted to seek cover and then Fritz lit his end of the fuse. The little flame turned into a fizzing glow that traveled along the forest floor at a surprising speed. That's when I jumped for shelter behind the fir and threw myself on the ground. It didn't take long until there came a terrific explosion. Bits and pieces of everything flew everywhere and rained down on everybody. When the breeze finally had cleared off the dust, there was no more stump. In fact there was nothing but a large shallow crater that smelled of burnt powder. We all came forward and danced around the hole, celebrating our grand victory.

During the following days, we produced a number of these bombs and blew up several more stumps. For every one of these stumps (enemy installations) that was blown up, one of us received another decoration.

*

Several days of rainy weather had kept us at home. When we were finally able to roam the woods again, we were ready for bigger things. The big event came when we decided to blow up a huge fir that we knew of. It was located near a limestone cave which had served us as base camp many times before. The tree was gigantic, but it was diseased and was dying. For us it became an enemy ammunition depot, a very important and valuable target. We had long since given up making decorations. Everyone had at least two or three Iron Crosses. This task, however, deserved something special. Each boy participating would become the proud owner of one of the famed "Ritterkreuz" (these were fashioned from double matches.)

We dumped the gun powder from several of the smaller cans into a sixty four ounce apple juice can. On the side furthest away from the cave, we started digging between two root legs of the mighty tree. It was a monumental job and we all took turns. Using the bayonet and our hands, the hole gradually progressed to the depth we thought would be sufficient. When the excavation was large enough, the can was placed under the tree, the end of the fuse inserted and the hole filled in again. We led the fuse around the trunk and played out enough to reach the mouth of the cave. All of us then assembled inside and sat down with our backs against the far wall. There we deemed ourselves safe from the expected shock wave, but we still had the base of the tree in full view.

It had taken four of us holding hands to encircle the trunk of the mighty fir. Even now, from ninety feet away, it still looked impressive. Helmut lit the fuse, ran back and settled down amongst us. Then we waited and waited, but nothing happened. We looked at each other and were puzzled. Our eyes were drawn back to the tree. No one wanted to miss the grand event, but still, nothing happened. Someone suggested that the fuse had gone out. This, however, had never happened to us before. The fuses had always kept fizzing even through moist grass and packed dirt.

"The dumb thing went out," Fritz mumbled, "I better check it."

"No! Let's wait some more, it couldn't have gone out," replied Helmut. He was a tall skinny teenager with brown short-cropped hair. His dark eyes were set deep in his pale face and he seldom laughed. Helmut was no coward, he just seemed more mature than Fritz, the other teenager.

"Okay, let's wait," consented Fritz with a sour grin on his face. Fritz seemed to be the opposite of Helmut in every way. He was built short and stocky with a thick shock of hair. His head was almost round and his ruddy face reminded me of a bulldog. His actions often seemed flighty and spontaneous. Both of them, however, had always treated us younger ones kindly and we trusted them. We now all agreed that we should wait some more. But when after two more minutes still nothing stirred, Helmut got up, saying "I'll redo the fuse." Some of us still tried to stop him. We pleaded with him to wait just a little longer, but Helmut too was by now convinced that the fuse had somehow failed. He walked to the entrance and inspected the trail of the burnt fuse.

Just then it happened: The explosion was horrendous. Helmut was thrown back into the cave, where he landed on the floor next to our feet. We also felt the shock wave, but with our backs pressed against the rocks we were not harmed. Debris blew into the cavern and pieces from the roof of our den rained down on us, but the cave survived. We were lucky once again, we could have all been buried. Helmut had a bloody nose, deep scratches on both legs and a goose egg formed on his forehead. Otherwise, he was fine. At home he would say that he fell into a cave, again, not a lie! The rest of us were unhurt.

The mighty tree stood as if nothing had happened, but around its roots the ground looked like a battlefield. Now, quite a discussion ensued. Why had it taken so long? The answer became obvious when Fritz checked the spool for the fuse. Somehow Helmut had gotten hold of a spool of the slow-burning kind. So far, we had always used the fuses marked "Fast" and were used to its speed.

But, there was another mystery for us: At the very first instant of the explosion, just before the dust cloud had developed, some of us had clearly seen the entire tree being lifted at least two feet off the ground. Then, it settled back down while the dust obliterated everything for quite some time. But, the enormous fir stood as if nothing had happened. This, of course, was highly improbable and hard to believe. Yet, we saw what we saw. The proof came about ten days later. After a heavy windstorm, we found the giant fir lying supine with its powder-blackened roots reaching helplessly into the clear morning sky. Even though it had been torn out of the ground, it had settled down in its old hole and had remained standing perfectly balanced. The next wind, however, was too much and it had fallen unnoticed by anyone. We then all accepted our "Ritterkreuz" and wore it proudly.

But alas, all good things must come to an end. Our school had been reorganized and once again we attended regular classes. Only now we were there for six hours a day and not just for two or three as before. Between homework and chores little time was left to roam the woods and our small band of little heroes soon broke up entirely.

In the years to follow, many such weapon caches had been found by farmers plowing their fields and on construction sites. But I am thoroughly convinced that quite a few of these supplies still remain in the ground undetected. The way these things were protected and sealed, they probably are quite well preserved and in fine condition to this very day.

Chapter Ten

At the Stake

Some very popular German writers of youth books had devoted several volumes to the North American Indian and especially their interactions with the earliest white trappers. There were stories of fierce battles amongst the different tribes, but also of true friendship between some Indians and some white men. Well known to every boy of that time were Karl May's books of Winnetou, the Apache chief. It was therefore only natural that our version of playing Cops and Robbers was "Playing Indians".

In the summer of 1945, a number of boys from our town got together and I suggested that we'd be Mohawks. Someone had given me a book with many stories about the Mohawk tribe. I had learned a lot about them and their chief, Wotawa. Since I owned the book, I became that chief, and was viewed as the authority on tribal life. The Indians were portrayed as honorable, proud, brave and fierce. We tried, of course, to live up to that reputation as best we could. The boys from a neighboring village had formed a similar band and called themselves Apaches. Winnetou was their chief.

Whenever we could get off, we met in the forest and played out our newfound roles. Most of the time we just made a lot of noise and had a good old time. But there were other aspects as well. We would make war against the Apaches, sneak up on them, take prisoners, bring them back to our camp and tie them to The Stake. At other times they did the same to us, but it usually ended by everyone amiably smoking the Peace Pipe. Whether these two tribes had ever actually met in real life, mattered little to us.

Some of us were armed, especially the chiefs. I had a short handled hatchet for my Tomahawk, several knives and one of my 6mm Flobert rifles. My mother knew nothing about my rifles, at least not at that time. I had always kept them well hidden. Had she known, she would have never allowed me to take them out for playing games.

One day, our Mohawks were ambushed. We had been completely unaware of the Apache's approach. The element of surprise was on their side and they took several of us for prisoners. I was amongst them and as Chief I was their prized catch. With great to-do, we were disarmed and marched several miles back to their camp. Once there, we were bound on hands and feet, as was the custom, and piled on the ground. I, being Chief, was tied to the trunk of a tree and was promised Torture at the Stake.

A Chief, according to our books, never showed fear and never complained under torture. I, however, had always been afraid of imminent pain and didn't at all know how well I would be able to play my role under these circumstances. As I leaned against the tree, they built a small fire near my feet. It was far enough away not to burn me, but it was so arranged that the smoke would be fully in my direction. While this was uncomfortable, I hoped that this would be the extent of their promised torture. I also hoped that my tears, caused by the smoke, would not be mistaken for crying.

While they held their palaver, no one paid much attention to us. They were far more interested in the weapons they had taken from us. Then, the calumet was brought out and handed around. Mohawks, however, were not included. That didn't look too good and we started to worry. But, according to Indian fashion, I leaned against the tree, ignored their occasional mocking remarks and stoically endured my burning eyes and the smoke.

The afternoon had worn on and daylight was beginning to fade. A couple of my braves began complaining and some started crying. All of my group were under strict orders from their mothers to be home before dark. Our captors, however, made no attempt of calling it a day. I addressed their chief and demanded that they let my buddies go. I bravely offered to stay instead since I was their prize catch. From my position, tied to the stake, I really didn't have much bargaining power. To my surprise, however, they agreed and let them go. Their weapons stayed, and so did I.

By now it was dark. The fire had been moved further away from me and it was built up into a roaring blaze. I knew I was in deep trouble. I should have been home by now. My mother was not exactly gentle with her punishments and I knew I wouldn't be able to sit straight for awhile after she'd got through with me. But there was nothing I could do about it. I intensely wished we could quit playing roles now, but unfortunately it was not up to me to initiate this.

Suddenly, I felt someone working on the ropes that held me. Whoever it was remained well hidden behind the big tree trunk. First the rope around my hands came free, then my feet and then I felt a knife-handle being pushed into my hands. I stood motionless. I remained like that for a few minutes to give my liberator a chance to get to safety, just as we had learned from our books. The Apaches paid no attention to me.

With a quick twist of my body I disappeared behind the tree and started running into the dark of the forest. However, in getting away I made entirely too much noise. I was no Indian.

They heard the noise I had made running and stumbling into trees, saw that I was gone and gave chase. They hollered I should stop or they'd shoot, but I kept running to the edge of the forest and out into a large clearing. While it had been quite dark within the trees, outside it was nearly as light as day. The full moon had risen unnoticed by us at the fire side. The clearing turned out to be a low meadow, a little boggy in places. A patch of low fog rested on the grass and into that I disappeared. I kept low and ran bent over because the fog was not high enough to hide me completely.

My pursuers had just reached the edge of the forest, when the shooting started. By the report of the gun I could tell it was a small caliber rifle, probably my own. There had been twelve bullets in the clip and they were coming fast. I couldn't stop; I was in too much trouble already, I had to get home. Not being very familiar with the area, I had to occasionally raise up to see where I was heading. Whenever I did that another bullet came flying and pretty close too. I had almost reached the far side of the clearing. I had to raise up one last time to look for a break in the thicket ahead that I could disappear into. That's when it got me. Hearing the shot and feeling the pain in my left knee were all in one. It felt like my knee was hit with a club and I went down. Having worn short pants, I could readily see the bleeding wound in the moonlight.

They found me soon enough. I could tell they were still deeply in their role as Indians. Since I couldn't walk, they dragged me back by my suspenders. There was nothing gentle about this and I tried my best to keep my bleeding knee from being dragged through the dirt. Back inside the forest, under the canopy of the trees, it was once again black as pitch until we reached the fire. They laid me down next to it, kicked the embers to make them flare up and looked at my wound. The bullet was visible just under the skin on the outside of my knee cap. The pain drove tears to my eyes which I desperately tried to hide from them. One of the older boys held his knife over the fire to sanitize it, as he called it.

"We'll fix you up," he mumbled, "should be no problem for a chief, right?" he added sarcastically.

Then, while someone held down my leg, he made two small cuts crosswise over the hole and with the point of his knife he popped the bullet out. It hurt so much I felt like passing out. Then he borrowed a shirt from one of their boys, tore off a sleeve and wrapped it around my knee. He cut off the other sleeve and handed it to me saying I might need it. He then helped me to my feet and told me to try and walk. I could not, of course. Their chief sent one of his braves to get his bicycle. The boy lived nearby and was back rather quickly. He was to give me a lift close to my home on the back of his bike.

The game was over and that's how we parted. I was in too much pain to worry about my gun and the other weapons they had taken from us. The bike ride was bumpy and painful. The boy dropped me off near my home and disappeared as fast as he could. I envied him for his bike. I had one too, but it had no tires and new ones were just not available.

The blood had come through my bandage. I removed it, hid it and wrapped the extra sleeve around my knee. Walking, by now, went better than I had imagined. I limped to our front door. Then on second thought, I took the bandage off again and hid it as well. I could have never explained where I had gotten it from.

When my mother saw me she was shocked. Naturally, she had been worried, but she had also worked up quite a rage at my unthinkable conduct. The whip had been laid at ready. Now, however, her immediate concern was my condition rather than my behavior. I thanked the Lord for that much! I realized that Mother probably acted in my best interest by always being so strict. I also was pretty certain that she loved me, but I often wished that she would be a little more like other mothers. A little less domineering, a little less haughty, not as strict and, finally, a little more understanding.

This time, I simply could not tell the truth. I told her I had fallen off a tree and that I had to pluck out a stone that had lodged in my knee. She wanted to call our family doctor to have him come and take care of me. Of course, I could not let that happen and fought that idea with all my wit. I knew he would not be fooled as easily and then I would really be in trouble.

Fortunately, my knee did not look near as bad as it felt. It was swollen a little, but the bleeding had almost stopped. My mother cleaned it up and bandaged it properly. She threatened that if it didn't look better in a day or two, she would fetch the doctor. The next morning, she even gave me a ride to school on the back of her bicycle. Yes, I got off easy. I had to think of the poor fellow that arrived home without his shirt sleeves. He was probably in far more trouble than I was. I hoped that his mother would not be as uncompromising as mine. Clothing was a scarce commodity. There was a whimsical saying in those days that it was better to have a hole in one's head than in one's breeches. The hole in the head would heal, the breeches wouldn't. It was not far from the generally prevailing attitude.

Word came to me that it had been none of our group that had freed me from the Stake. It must have been one of the others that perhaps had felt sorry for me. I never did find out who it was. My knee healed surprisingly fast. No lasting damage had been done, the scar, however, remains to this day. While my leg was mending I was not allowed to go into the woods. I worried about my gun and the other things that had been taken from us. We had gotten along reasonably well with the boys from the other village, but in playing our roles as chiefs and warriors, our relationship had always become something drastically different. As soon as I was able to sneak away, I went to see them about our stuff. To my great relief there were no problems. They were as glad about my speedy recovery as I was. I got everything back that they had taken and the whole thing was resolved amiably.

There were only three cartridges left in my rifle. I really had been shot by my own gun. Things like this would be totally unthinkable during normal times. These, however, were not normal times.

Chapter Eleven

The Hunt

Most everything had been on rations for years.
These rations, however, were so meager that an average person could not possibly survive on them. Also,
even with ration cards, things could only be bought
whenever they happened to be available at the different stores. Many hours were spent standing in long
lines on the side walk in front of the bakery, for instance, only to be told that the last loaf of bread had
just been sold.

Everyone had to somehow try to do something, one
way or the other, to supplement these rations. People
living in the suburbs or in the country were able to
plant gardens. City people were not that fortunate.
Little could be done, however, to obtain additional meat.
Every head of cattle, every hog, goat or sheep was registered with the authorities. Farmers were not allowed
to butcher anything without proper permits and then
only under strict supervision. Of course, a lot of illegal
butchering *did* take place, but the proceeds from these
never trickled down to the general population. Instead
it disappeared in "Black Market" activities, enriching
the lives of farmers and smooth-talking, slick opera-
tors.

Once the war was over, this changed somewhat.
The rations did not get any better, but there was, for
awhile at least, no law enforcement to worry about.
The woods were full of deer, hares and rabbits. Unfortunately, most people had given up all their guns and
rifles as ordered by the American Forces. My mother,

145

fearing reprisals, had dutifully taken all my grandfather's hunting guns, our handguns and even my little small caliber rifle to town and had surrendered them to the authorities. She was promised that, in time, we would get them back. But that was an outright lie. To identify them later, Mother had carved our name prominently into every stock, but we never saw them again. Much later, we found out that every one of these guns had gone State-side as personal property of some officer or soldier.

Now, we were completely unarmed, except for the two small Floberts, which I had secured one night from the Volkssturm cache. But, I had kept them well hidden. One day, Mother complained that if we still had our guns we could try to poach a deer some night. This seemed a good time for me to confess about my treasure. I only mentioned one of them and told her I had found it in the woods, along with several boxes of ammunition. At first she was quite angry. However, when I pointed out that without the gun there could be no venison, she began to see it from a different angle.

Mother began to ask all kinds of questions. Did I know where to find deer? Would anyone be able to hear the shot? Could I get it home without being seen and without someone robbing me of my loot? Of course, I stilled her concerns and assured her that there would be no problems. She was never really against doing something like that, her main concern seemed to be not to get caught at it.

One afternoon, while I was doing my homework, Mother brought me a plate with what I thought was chocolate pudding. But alas, it was no pudding. She had scraped out some pork liver, sprinkled some salt and pepper over it and had heated it in the oven until a light skin had formed over it. She told me to eat it. I tried it, but I almost gagged. I didn't like it. She explained that it would improve my night vision, since I was supposed to get a deer for us that night. Now, that was different.

"You mean you'll let me go hunting?" I blurted out.

"Yes, if you promise to be very careful," she replied, "we don't want anything to happen. And, of course, nobody is to know about this." she added. I couldn't believe my good fortune. Coming from her, this really was a surprise. Of course, we both knew that neither Mom nor Dad were hunters. It was up to me.

I made myself think of pudding, forced the virtually raw liver down and hoped it would stay there. Then Mother brought dessert. She had chopped raw carrots and, knowing that I didn't much care for vegetables, had sprinkled some sugar over it. Someone had told her that these things are good for one's eyes and that they would temporarily improve one's night vision. Apparently she believed in it. I didn't care one way or the other as long as I could go hunting that night.

During the last couple of years of the war, my grandfather, who was an avid hunter, had taken me with him on his hunts many times. He had taught me how to shoot and the fundamentals of hunting. He also had presented me with a small-caliber rifle of my own, which, alas, had been amongst the ones my mother had so dutifully delivered to the American authorities. Grandpa used to have two hunting leases and had allowed me to kill deer on my own. My greatest accomplishment had been the killing of a mature, male elk when I was only nine years old. I did have some experience.

I got one of my rifles from it's hiding place and began to carefully clean it, using the oil of mother's sewing machine. I hoped it would only take one shot, but I filled the entire clip, just in case. Now I was ready. The rest of the afternoon dragged on endlessly; I thought it would never get dark. When it finally did, she gave me some dark clothes to wear and I camouflaged my face with some soot from the stove. I still had to wait for total darkness.

It was past ten o'clock by now. We shut off the light in the living room and, after receiving more reminders not to get hurt and not to get caught, I stepped out into the night. I always did have surprisingly good night vision, but this was phenomenal! There was no moon and the stars were behind clouds, but to me it was as bright as if there had been a full moon that had just gone behind some thin clouds. There were, of course, no distinct shadows and their absence confused me for a moment, but I could see everything as never before at night. Besides my gun, I wore my grandfathers Rucksack, which is the German name for a large backpack, and his hunting knife.

I headed for a clearing in the forest that I knew to be frequented by deer. The succulent grass, the young sapling and the nearness of the protecting forest made it ideal habitat for them. The European deer are a rather small species. They are called roebucks and are only the size of sheep, just a little taller.

It was about a thirty minute walk, but my vision was so improved that I had no problem finding my way in the darkness of the forest. When I arrived at the clearing, there were no deer. They either had not yet shown up or my approach had spooked them. Whatever it was, I settled down at the edge of the forest and made myself comfortable. I sat on the backpack and leaned against a large tree trunk. It was a balmy late-summer night. There was no breeze and the forest was silent. It was a long wait and doubts started to creep up about my choice of location. But I had gambled on this place and would stick with it until daybreak.

Then fatigue started to catch up with me. My eye-lids became heavy and several times I caught myself sitting there with my eyes closed. I hoped I could stay awake. Knowing that I couldn't move, I made my eyes rove in every direction to keep my mind occupied. Then I thought I saw a faint movement at the far side of the clearing. Yes, there stood a deer. As it stepped further into the open, another one came and joined it. Then there were three, four, five and so on until a small herd had assembled. I was no longer tired. Now they were starting to graze. Slowly, I picked up my rifle that had rested across my legs and carefully removed the safety.

I picked out a doe that seemed slightly larger than the rest of them. I had an unobstructed view and could have shot then and there, but I wanted a closer shot. After all, my rifle was only a small caliber gun. I didn't trust its knock-down power at such a distance. A wounded deer, limping off into the forest, was the last thing I needed that night. The herd was slowly graz-ing across the clearing and their present course would soon bring them closer to me. But without any breeze at all, I did not know how close I could let them come before they'd detect me. I had always preferred to be down-wind of my quarry, but that could not be helped now.

While grazing, the deer had scattered some, mak-ing it easier to pick out an individual target without hurting a second one. Then the larger doe raised her head and seemed to be looking in my direction. I froze, I didn't even dare to breathe. Finally her head went down and she continued grazing. The time had come. Ever so slowly, I raised my rifle, aimed for her low shoulder and fired. The deer dropped instantly and after a few feeble kicks of it's hind legs it lay still. So did I. Not knowing who might have heard the shot or who else might be out at night, I had to be very careful. So I just laid low and waited.

After a long wait, there was some noise to the left, but it was only from the other deer. The herd had scattered, after the shot, but now they returned and looked at their fallen friend. It seemed they could not understand why she didn't come along with them. They were slowly milling around and even sniffed at their dead comrade. This told me that there was no one else around and that it was at last perfectly safe to pick up my prize. At my slightest movement the deer vanished. I walked over to my quarry and carefully checked for any signs of life. There were none. As was customary, I took my knife and cut the side of its throat to let it bleed. I sat down on her rib-cage and waited. It was then that I realized that my hands were shaking. The excitement finally had taken hold of me. From prior hunts I was familiar with this sensation. It was not an uncomfortable feeling, so I just sat there and let it happen. Gradually it wore off and gave way to a feeling of deep satisfaction. I had gone on a mission, I had succeeded, and now I could go home.

The doe was a big one. It didn't quite fit into my backpack, the head and front legs were still hanging out. It also was a lot heavier than I had anticipated, but I was strong and my pride certainly helped with carrying the cumbersome burden. I was about two miles from home. To keep my balance, I had to walk deeply bent over under my heavy load. I had to rest quite often. Mainly, because of the weight, but also to listen. If someone would have caught me, my prize and my weapons would have been taken away and I would have been chased home empty-handed. That is if I was lucky. A lot worse things had been happening to children in those days, things I didn't care to think about at that moment. Several times I had to readjust the straps on my pack to get it into a more comfortable position.

Finally, I reached the back fence of our property and within two more minutes I arrived at our door. Mother had waited up for me. She walked me to the basement door and there helped me out of my pack. Together we dragged it inside. She had covered the window with old blankets. She waited until the door was shut and securely locked, before she switched on the light. One had to be so careful, jealous and envious neighbors were never far. I helped her hang the deer by its hind feet and started to skin it out, just as Grandpa had taught me. Mother, however, said she'd be all right and sent me to bed. I had to go to school in the morning after all. I went upstairs, got cleaned up and went to bed.

Sleep, however, was slow in coming. Yes, I was tired – worn out is a better word – but my mind kept going back to my experience. How soon would I be allowed to go hunting again? Where would I find my quarry the next time? I eventually did drop off. The next morning, I had an especially rough time getting out of bed. To make things worse, I couldn't even talk or brag about my successful hunt to my buddies in school. Somehow I truly missed that, but it couldn't be helped.

When I came home that afternoon, Mom was still busy pulling skins off the various meat pieces. Some she had prepared for our next few meals. Some she was fixing to age, but most of it she would cook and preserve in glass jars, similar to the fruits and vegetables she had put up. I didn't care much about the details, as long as there was venison to eat. We preferred it to any other meat.

There were several other times when I was sent poaching. I loved it even when, at times, I was not successful in finding game. Mostly, however, luck was with me. Not only did I enjoy the hunt and the excitement of having to do it in secrecy, I also saw myself a little as our provider.

Chapter Twelve

A Close Call

I vividly remember a cold, moonlit January night of 1946. My parents had company that evening. When I happened to look out of the bathroom window, I saw the full moon above lighting up the snow-covered land-scape. It was a picture of such loveliness that I wanted nothing more than to be out there in the stillness of the night, riding my sled. I entered our little living-room and waited for a pause in the adult's conversation. Then I asked Mother if I could go out and ride my sled.

"Sure, go ahead," she replied, but she seemed pre-occupied with her company. I suspected that, though she had heard me, she really hadn't been listening. It was ten thirty and normally she would have never agreed to my silly request. But that was fine with me, I had asked and she had allowed it. Cautiously leav-ing the room, I only hoped Mother wouldn't reconsider before I was gone.

I put on my boots and my coat, eased out the front door and picked up my sled from under the bench in the basement. I crossed our orchard and climbed our back fence. After I traversed the railroad tracks, I pulled my little sled up over some gently sloping pas-tures. I headed for a patch of forest a quarter of a mile ahead at the end of the field. The moonlit night seemed as bright as day and the air was crystal-clear. Looking around, I felt enchanted by the sheer beauty of that night. The serenity of the scene made it seem as if the peacefulness of Christmas still lingered on out here in this tranquil countryside. The clean, undisturbed snow was covered with a frozen crust which reflected the moonlight like millions of little stars. By walking gingerly this crust would just support my weight. This made my progress quite effortless. Only occasionally did I break through into the knee-deep, powdery snow below. Reaching the end of the field, I followed an indistinct, curving trail which snaked its way through the forest. After some three-hundred yards, it would end at a gravel road at the far side of the trees. By now, the trail had completely disappeared under the deep snow, but I navigated between the trees by memory and followed it just the same. Walking through the quiet moonlit forest, I imagined myself as secretive and as shy as a deer. That thought pleased me somehow and I smiled. The terrain inside the forest was much steeper than it had been out on that sloping pasture and I had almost worked up a sweat when I reached the little road.

I rested to catch my breath and relished the crisp coldness of the night on my face. Looking to my right, the road led into town. To the left I knew it would soon end after reaching the last few lonely houses that were spread out on the hillside. On the opposite side, however, another little short lane started up a very steep and curved grade. I decided I would climb to its summit. I knew that after about a hundred yards, there would be another crossroad up there. I planned to ride down from there two times, stopping each time at this lower crossing where I stood now. Then I planned to lay on my sled, relax and look up at the moon for awhile. After that, I would climb up there once more. On that third and last time, I would not stop here. Instead, I would keep on riding across the road, through the forest, down over the field and all the way home.

Doing just what I had planned, I enjoyed those two short rides tremendously. Then I laid down on my sled, got comfortable and looked at that beautiful, full moon. I wasn't lying there for even a minute, when suddenly I felt an uneasiness creeping up. It was like an inner feeling, telling me to forget about looking at the moon, to climb to the top and race home as fast as I could. It all was as clear as an inner voice talking to me. Bewildered, I followed this notion immediately. As I was about halfway up the steep slope, I suddenly heard footsteps crunching on the frosty ground below me. I turned around and saw a dark figure approaching. It was at the lower part of the lane which was still within the shadows of nearby trees. I stopped, trying to make out who or what it was that came up the slope behind me, but I realized that as long as it was still in the shade it would be impossible to identify.

I proceeded up the hill, looking back occasionally. As the road bent and the figure stepped into the full moonlight, I recognized that it was a man wearing one of those dreaded inmate-caps and Russian-type boots. That was all I needed to send me on my way to the top in a hurry. Arriving there, I turned my sled around, sat on it and pushed off. The closer the stranger came, the scarier he looked. My sled had started to move and was just picking up speed, when I steered to the right to let him pass on my left. He apparently saw that and stepped to my right, blocking my way. I steered left, but he also jumped to that side. My sled had gathered some speed by now and I decided to steer directly for him, hoping he would eventually step aside. He did, but he bent down, one hand reaching for me, while his other hand wielded something long and shiny that reflected in the moonlight. I couldn't tell if it was a knife or just a length of pipe. Instinctively, I had let myself drop backwards to lie on my sled. His groping hand missed me, clutching empty air instead. The speed of my sled whisked me by him. In some harsh, alien sounding language, he snarled something that sounded like *yoobént*.

Now, I had to pay full attention not to miss the bend of the lane. When I had that under control, I looked back and saw him, as he was running after me. Moving at full speed I disappeared into the shady part of the lane. Then my sled and I came flying across that moonlit intersection, heading for the forest. I heard someone shriek. Glancing over my shoulder, I spotted a couple of men on their way home from town. My sudden appearance must have startled them and I heard one of them declare he had thought I was a deer. I didn't stop.

I was in full flight and kept on going. The curvy path through the forest was marked by my earlier shallow footprints. At this speed, however, it demanded my full attention and only as I reached the open field could I relax a little. The sled stayed on top of that icy crust and I enjoyed the tremendous speed. I relished being compared to a deer, it reminded me of my earlier fantasy. As I swiftly reached the railroad tracks, I steered into a sharp left-hand slide and came to rest next to the tall embankment. I pulled the sled up to the tracks, looking back the way I had come. I could see as far as the edge of the forest, but nobody could be seen following me. I climbed our fence and on crossing our orchard, admired its beauty in the moonlight.

I put my sled away, knocked the snow off my feet and walked in. Our company had just left. I was eager to tell my parents what had happened, but before I could say one word, Mother charged at me, "Where have you been?"

"I was out riding my sled," I replied.

"What," she screamed, "in the middle of the night? Are you crazy?"

"No," I defended myself, "I asked you if I could go and you said it was all right."

"You never asked me," she stormed, "When did you ask?"

"When you were talking to your guests," I offered.

"You never asked me anything," she insisted, "you know quite well I wouldn't have allowed it. Now get to bed."

The fact that I didn't get whipped showed me that she wasn't really sure about the whole affair. At any rate, I thought it wise not to mention my scary experience at that time and disappeared into the bedroom without any further delay.

Before I fell asleep, I pondered over the night's events. I asked myself where this inner warning had come from that I had heard so clearly, and what would have happened had I ignored that warning. So far, I hadn't really felt threatened, but I knew instinctively that it had been a close call. I didn't find out till much later just how close it really was and what would have probably happened to me. Right then, I only mused what the phrase *"yoobént"* might have meant. I wondered if he had tried to speak English. I did have English classes in school for about a half a year now and had learned enough to know what *you bent* meant. That would have made some sense. I *had* bent to avoid his grasp, but why would he speak in English to me? It was probably some cuss-word in his native language (to this day, I have never found the answer.) Then, somewhat exhausted, I fell asleep.

Chapter Thirteen

Who Needs Money?

It was now spring of 1946. For several years, trading and bartering had become the standard of survival. Everyone seemed to have some money, but in reality no one wanted it. One could not eat money. People who had a trade and could fix or repair something were relatively well off. They would not work for money, but if one promised them some groceries they would be there to take care of whatever had broken down. Intellectuals, on the other hand, were usually on the brink of starvation. The general public did not need their knowledge during those meager times. With few exceptions, these highly educated individuals fared even worse than the rest of us. The only exception to my personal knowledge was a university professor who came twice a week to teach English to my mother. For each lesson, he would accept a couple of eggs, or a few sandwiches, or three or four American cigarettes. He did have a few other clients as well.

I vividly remember my first personal experience in bartering which, at the same time, turned into my first lesson in successful negotiation. It had been shortly after Mother and I had moved to Starnberg in October of 1943. Mother had suggested that I should learn to ride a bicycle. I was eight years old then and all in favor of it, but we didn't own a child's bike. There was no chance of buying one either, they were simply not available. All factories had been refitted to produce war materials exclusively. Mother, however, owned an old full-size lady's bike and this was what I had to use. A gravel walkway along our back fence became my training track.

The bike was huge and awkward, way too big for my little body. Standing on the pedals, with my arms raised high above my head, my hands could barely grasp the handle bar. While Mother jogged alongside, hanging on to the baggage carrier in the back, I pumped the pedals. I steered as well as I could with the point of the saddle bumping me between my shoulders. Unable to sit in the saddle I had very little balance control. It was all right as long as Mom ran beside me and hung on, but the minute she thought it safe to let go I started to wobble and fell.

Many evenings we practiced. I was just beginning to gain some confidence, proudly noticing that Mom was no longer holding on when disaster struck. The gravel path had a steady downhill slope and was straight for about a hundred yards. Then it turned abruptly to the right and continued straight again. In my confidence I had let the speed build up, leaving Mom way behind. When I reached the curve, I realized that I was going much too fast and slammed on the brake. Too late. The path turned to the right, I did not. Mom had to pull me and the bike out of the bushes. Besides minor cuts, scrapes and bruises, no major harm was done. Since I had no other choice, I just kept at it and soon I became proficient enough to go out on my own.

I enjoyed the new freedom the bike provided. It was a twenty-five minute walk from our house into town, now I could be there in less than five minutes. But alas, there were strings attached to this newfound independence. From now on I had to do most of the daily grocery shopping. Mom would give me the appropriate ration cards and some money and send me to stand in the long lines in front of each store. But I didn't mind. I became quite efficient riding that oversized bicycle with bags hanging off each side of the handle bars and a bucket containing a quart of milk in my hand. But I always envied any boy fortunate enough to own a smaller bike, and for being able to comfortably sit on the saddle.

Then, one fine spring morning in 1944, Mrs. Stamm came to visit us. Her son was one of my class mates. She was a tall, stern woman who talked with an overly loud voice. Her jet-black hair was piled up on top of her head and when she did smile, her teeth showed white and even. To me she seemed overpowering and I was a little afraid of her. But she had graciously allowed me to visit them once a week to practice on their piano. Since we had been bombed out in Munich, I had, for a short while, continued piano lessons in Starnberg. We had, however, no longer an instrument to practice on since our piano had been destroyed by bombs along with all our other belongings in the city.

In the course of conversation, Mrs. Stamm mentioned that she urgently needed a good bicycle pump. What she actually had in mind was one of the bigger and sturdier pumps designed for automobiles. She said she would be willing to trade her son's boy-sized bicycle for it. I couldn't believe what I had heard and in my eagerness I innocently blurted out,

"Mom, lets do it! There are about six of these pumps stored in the shed back there and I need a smaller bike."

Mom shot me one of her angry glances, which shut me up instantly. She swiftly amended my thoughtless outburst, saying that there possibly might be such a pump and steered the conversation to the small bicycle. We found out that the bike was in good shape except that the tires had been substituted with solid-rubber replacements. At that point, I didn't care about the tires and the deal was agreed upon.

After our visitor had left, Mom called me into the bedroom. She was furious and came down hard on me because of my inexcusable and stupid behavior, as she called it.

"You must never tell anyone what's back there in the shed," she yelled, "Mainly, you should never let on that something the other party wants is easily available. That will only cause them to drive a harder bargain and ask for more. You can indicate that, perhaps, you might be able to put your hands on whatever it is that they need. I hope you understand that now," she continued. "One more incident like this and I'll spank you till your hide comes off!"

I got the message and was only glad that I didn't get whipped this time. Thus went my first lesson in negotiating and bartering.

The next day, we delivered the pump and picked up the bike. It fit me perfectly and I was delighted. Upon riding it, however, I soon began to dislike those tire-imitations. They were made of little hard rubber disks strung on a wire like pearls on a necklace and then rolled onto the rims. They caused an excessively bumpy ride which had to be quite hard on the rims and spokes. But, I soon got used to it and found out that at higher speeds, it wasn't so bad. When driving slow, however, it vibrated so bad that it rattled my teeth. It didn't take very long and these tire imitations broke up completely, spilling rubber disks all over the road. That was the end of my bike and I had to ride Mom's again. Our store in Munich never carried bicycle parts or accessories and we had no source for tires. Bicycle tires, just like whole bikes, were no longer manufactured.

*

Now, three years later, bartering was still going strong. Many other ways to supplement meager rations had become the norm. One could trade valuables for food, if one was fortunate to still have any. In our case, Mother and I had planted a rather large garden. We raised vegetables, potatoes, beets and all kinds of berries. Our orchard provided us with apples, pears, plums and hazel nuts. It was a lot of work. Neither Mother, a business woman, nor I were used to that kind of toil, but we learned fast. Soon, Mother bought thirty freshly hatched chicks and we learned to raise them to get eggs and meat. We put five ducks on our pond and used their eggs for cooking.

In a little house near the railroad tracks lived an old man with his family. They owned a cow and needed hay to feed it. For letting him cut our grass, he would on occasions give us a quart or two of milk to supplement our meager rations. When the old man passed away, the cow was sold and we were once again out of milk. Mom, in desperation, traded some auto parts for a goat. We had converted one of our outbuildings into a barn and it housed our little menagerie comfortably. When Dad came home from the war, we obtained a second goat. He needed the nourishing milk to get his strength back. The goats were staked out all over our property to eat grass shrubs and assorted plants, but they still needed additional feed, especially during the long winters months.

Chapter Fourteen

Errands in the Night

One fine summer afternoon of 1946, my parents sent me on a special errand. In the next valley lived a Mr. Summer, the owner of a restaurant. He also owned a butcher shop. He was suspected of Black Market activities and his house had been closely watched for years. However, the man had been careful and lucky, he was never caught.

There had always been only a fine line between bartering and actual Black Market operations, but in a lot of instances this line was barely recognizable. Although the war was over one still had to be very careful with such enterprises. Less fortunate people were extremely jealous and envious. They would either turn you in to the law or even try to acquire any goods so observed for themselves if they could.

I was supposed to meet with this man and pick up a hundred pounds of grain to feed our goats, and a large section of meat for our table. I was to leave during daylight hours, but was to wait in the forest until well after dark before approaching his place.

When the time came, I left with our rather large hand-wagon with its stake-like sides. The wagon itself was a rare and much coveted commodity that could be easily taken from a child. I had to be quite wary, especially on the little travelled back roads which I would have to use. A long trip lay before me. The first part was mostly uphill, but the empty wagon was not much of a problem. Then I had to cross through a large forest of pines. There was a gravel path along the edge

165

of the forest, but I preferred to walk amongst the trees, carefully picking my way between the tall trunks.

As I finally reached the end of the forest I stopped before emerging into the open. This seemed as good a place as any to wait for darkness. Before me lay an open downhill slope and on its far end I could see the house of the man I was supposed to meet. It was already dusk and I realized I wouldn't have to wait too much longer. I looked around — and froze. There, between some tree-trunks, I saw the silhouette of a man. He was also standing near the edge of the forest. He wore the cap of one of these dreaded camp inmates and a short pipe stuck out of his mouth. After getting over my first scare, I looked closer to see if I had been detected. I felt certain that I had been spotted. The figure stood motionless. But all I could make out was a quartering profile and I couldn't be sure if he looked towards or away from me.

Suddenly, an awful memory resurfaced. My mind flashed back to the close call I had encountered last winter and panic threatened to overwhelm me. Again I saw the man that had tried to grab me and compared it to what I saw now. It all seemed so similar. I prayed that it wouldn't come to another such confrontation.

After a long time of staring, hope slowly returned to me that I hadn't been seen after all and I calmed down a little. I decided to ease backwards and out of sight. Leaving the wagon, I inched back step by careful step, never taking my eyes from him. As I put my foot down again, a twig snapped. It sounded like a pistol shot in the stillness of the forest. The stranger heard it and jerked. Now he saw me and with a small yell he took off running and didn't come back. Immediately, I felt quite big, having a grown man run away from me was the last thing I had expected. Apparently he had been facing away from me and had been totally unaware of my presence. When that dreaded twig snapped under my weight, he spotted me and took off. It showed me that I was not the only one that was nervous.

I repositioned the wagon and myself farther along the edge of the forest, found a comfortable spot with a clear view and sat down to rest. Slowly, as I watched, the shadows descended and it grew dark. The spacious pasture before me gently sloped away, framed by some rolling hills in the background. In spite of the darkness I could clearly see the house on the far side half tucked under a copse of large trees. Behind it was the highway. There was no traffic on it at this late hour. It was a peaceful and quiet scene, but I found no comfort in it. Soon I would have to cross that open area and I felt vulnerable and naked.

As soon as I deemed it was dark enough, I left the protection of the forest and made straight for the house. Mr. Summer had been waiting for me. A whispered greeting was exchanged and he ushered me into the dark hallway. He was a man of quick movements and in his forties. His round face was of a reddish hue and he had hard, staring eyes. I followed him to the far corner where, under a tarp, he had my stuff ready. He pulled back the cover and by the light of a flashlight showed me a large side of meat and a sack full of grain. He wrapped the meat with the tarp and together we carried everything to the door. He extinguished his flashlight, opened the door and carefully peered outside.

"Let's go," he hissed. We put the stuff onto the wagon, with the heavy sack covering the wrapped meat.

Before I knew it, I heard the door shut behind me and he was gone. I was on my own.

I thought back to the first time I had seen that man. He had come to our house only a few days ago. Dad had somehow acquired several pairs of German leather army boots. This man had shown an interest in those boots and a deal had been struck. He had taken the boots with him and had driven off in his car. It was one of the rare automobiles registered to civilians in those days. You had to know somebody to get the necessary permits and you had to have something besides the fees. This man apparently had come up with what it had taken.

Although I had carefully greased the axles of the wagon, before I left home, I soon found out that the heavy burden caused the wagon to creak and even squeak at times. To pull the weighty load up that sloping pasture was hard work. What wore me down worse, however, was the fear of being caught in the open. It wasn't contraband that I carried, but honestly paid-for goods, yet they were in high demand and some people would do just about anything to get a hold of my treasure.

Frequently, I stopped to rest and to listen, but all remained quiet. When I finally reached the corner of the forest, I pulled the wagon into the protection of the trees and rested for a long time. Nothing stirred. When I had calmed down and rested enough, I decided, that since it was dark, I would make better speed on the road along the edge of the forest. Upon reaching it, however, I found that the noise of the wheels on all that gravel would be loud enough to alert the whole countryside. So, after a short while, I opted for the stillness of the woods, where the wheels rolled noiselessly over the mossy forest floor. By staying close to the edge, I had sufficient light left to travel by, feeling my way between the tree trunks whenever necessary. Then I overlooked a stump and I went sprawling. The floor was soft, but I cruelly hurt my shin bone on that stump. The wagon rolled backwards down the slope, until it crashed into a tree and stopped. No damage was done, but my leg hurt badly. I decided once again to risk the road, but the noise was as bad as before. However, I soon found out that there was enough room for the wagon if I just stayed between the gravel and the edge of the forest. Here the noise was greatly reduced.

So I trudged on, mainly uphill, until I came to a cross road. Here I would have to turn to the right. Carefully I approached the intersection, listening in all directions, but nothing stirred. From now on, I had to be extra cautious because there would be no place to hide or to duck into. This road was lined with picket fences on both sides. It was so dark that I couldn't see any of the small bungalows, that I knew lay hidden by shrubs behind those fences. At this time of night, there were no lights on in any of them. I envied the people in their comfortable beds, while I had to trudge on. My leg hurt so much it, almost made me careless in my desire to get home and to bed. Luckily, the wagon didn't make quite as much noise on this road. Though the terrain was more level now, I had to rest frequently. I walked on for a long time, but I just had to rest again.

Right in the middle of the road I stopped and sat myself on the rails of the wagon to relieve my tired, aching legs. Then I heard footsteps. From behind me, I saw a man coming down the road right for me. There was no time to move the wagon aside, it would have made too much noise. I hoped his night vision would not be as keen as mine and that he would pass right by. I was only half right. He would have never seen me, but he bumped smack into the back of the wagon.

"What the —," he started as he tripped, then he saw me. "What in Heaven's name are you doing out here in the middle of the night?" he hollered.

"Waiting for my dad and my uncle," I lied. "They just went over there," I motioned vaguely with my arm, "to check something out."

"I sure wish you'd had a light," he complained.

"Dad has got the light with him," I replied, hoping for the best. Without another word he proceeded on his way.

'Wow, that was close,' I thought, wiping the sweat off my face. I gave him plenty of time to be far ahead of me, before I started walking again. Soon the road began to slope downhill, until I had to turn off again. Now I had only a small section of forest to cross, until I would come to the railroad tracks near our home.

The wagon made no noise on the mossy floor of the forest and going downhill made it easy for me. My thoughts strayed back to the incident on the road back there. I was surprised how easily that man had been fooled. He may have been perfectly harmless, but I had thought it prudent not to let on that I was alone. At least, I had escaped a bunch of awkward questions, if nothing worse.

The last part of the trip lay in front of me. I let the wagon roll beside me as I was crossing a recently mowed, downhill pasture. Reaching the railroad, I hid the wagon in some bushes, climbed the embankment, crossed the tracks, crawled through a hole in our back fence and ran to our door. Mom and Dad had been waiting for me. After assuring them that all had gone well, I led them to our wagon. The three of us worked together to get the heavy load over the tracks and into our house without being seen. Then it was time for me to get to bed. Although my leg was still hurting where I skinned my shin, I fell asleep almost instantly.

I made a few more trips like that in the months to come. I got used to it and it almost became routine. I never got caught and never had anything taken from me. However, I was quite glad as times gradually changed, making such endeavors unnecessary. With the devaluation of the German currency in 1948, things quickly normalized and bartering soon became history.

Chapter Fifteen

Cravings

Many former German P.O.W.s were wandering the streets on their way home to their families. Most of them had escaped from the Russian camps. The Russians had not even begun to release their prisoners except for a few that were in such bad health that they weren't expected to live another month. When we heard how miserable these men had been treated, we were once again thankful to be living in what had turned out to be the American Occupation Zone.

American P.O.W. camps, according to my father, had been run very efficiently and humanely. The German soldiers in most of these camps had been treated decently and with respect, and they were being released rather quickly. There was, however, one exception: We had heard of one American P.O.W. camp where things were apparently quite different. It was located near Bad Kreuznach, a peaceful town in a sleepy little side valley of the Rhine river basin. Reports had filtered out that the German prisoners there were being severely mistreated. They were starved on one small cup of watery soup per day. The inadequate hygiene facilities had caused numerous outbreaks of typhus and cholera. It was said that the commander was a convinced German-hater who ran the facility like a concentration camp. Countless German P.O.W.s died there needlessly at the hands of this fiend. But, I still think this had been an extreme exception. There are, however, many who insist that Bad Kreuznach was not an isolated case and that about a half a million former German soldiers had needlessly died of exposure and malnutrition in American and French P.O.W. camps such as Bad Kreuznach and others like it. However, I have no personal knowledge of this. By and large, the Americans became known as benevolent, tolerant and gracious people.

German soldiers that had been captured by the Russians, however, had not been that fortunate. Many of them were literary worked to death in underground salt mines, others were taken to Siberia to perform forced labor for many years to come. A staggering number of German soldiers are still missing and unaccounted for to this day.

We helped these poor wretches wherever we could. Often we shared what little food we had with them and afterwards gave them an American cigarette. One fellow, a mere skeleton of a man, after he had eaten with us and had enjoyed his cigarette, disappeared into our woods behind the house. We figured he'd be resting in the shaded grass under the trees. But soon we heard the noise of someone chopping firewood. We walked back there to see what was going on. The man had taken the hatchet out from where it had been wedged into the block and had started chopping up the branches that we had piled there earlier. We told him he didn't have to do that, but he only smiled and went on. He didn't quit until it got dark. We invited him in for supper. He gladly accepted. When we asked him what we owed him for his work, he asked if we could spare him one more cigarette. That was all he wanted. While they were all in need of decent food and clothing, it was their constant craving for tobacco that never failed to amaze me.

German men were picking up American cigarette butts wherever they could find them. They would tear the paper open and collect the remaining tobacco. When they had enough together they would roll them in fresh paper, often using the clean rim of old newspapers, and happily smoke their homemade treasure. When a GI threw away his still lit butt, it was not uncommon to see some man running for it to pick it up. He would then smoke it until it was so short that he could not hold on to it any longer. Even then, the remaining tobacco was collected for future use.

*

There was never any compensation for what my parents had lost due to the war. What was worse, Dad had lost title to the property in Munich where his business had once been. By June of 1945, many city administrations had ordered all women from the age of 15 to 50, to participate in the removal of the rubble of their cities. The women received forty Reichs Mark per week (the equivalent of four cigarettes.) The means of enforcing compliance with this cleanup operation was highly effective. Those who did not work, received no ration cards. The expense of this operation was charged back to the different property owners or, since a lot of them had perished, to their heirs. If they were unable to pay, they lost title to their property. As cleanup operations in Munich had started to get underway, a simple form-letter from the city of Munich ordered my Dad to have the rubble removed from his property and the lot cleared off completely. Dad, who had just returned from the war, severely wounded, did not have the money or the resources to get this done. The city ended up doing it for him and charged him for it. Since he couldn't pay, the city took title to the site and called it even.

Dad had miraculously survived the two gut-shots from the war and they gave him relatively little discomfort. He knew he had to start his business again. But, for that he needed capital. Taking up credit or borrowing had always been unthinkable for my parents. What they couldn't pay for with cash or by trading, they did without. Too many ill feelings had been born in pre-war Germany between parasiting money-lenders on one hand, and poor, helpless citizens on the other. The interest rates had been astronomical. All too soon, these desperate borrowers had found out that once in debt, they would never again be able to get out of debt. The only solution my parents could think of now was to sell a parcel of our land.

When I heard about this, my heart was saddened and I found it difficult to accept. But I had no say in the matter and I supposed it had to be done. The park-like grounds with its majestic trees, orchards and meadows had been my paradise. I was equally fond of our pond and the low, boggy area surrounding it. But to my parents, these low areas were useless acreage that had no value, unless they were filled in.

The first attempts of rebuilding Munich were being undertaken. Of paramount priority, however, had been the removal of the rubble. Any solution seemed right, at that time. A huge mountain started appearing in a park within the city limits. People referred to it as Mt. Rubble. The unfinished subway tunnels, that had been dug out before the war and had served as bomb shelters during the war, were now filled in with the rubble. Anything, just to get rid of it, as fast as possible. Whoever needed fill-dirt had only to say the word and truckload after truckload would appear, by day and by night.

Dad made use of this and soon hundreds of truck-loads of city rubble started to pile up on our land, filling in our pond and the lower areas. A dozer and his operator pushed dirt around for days to make room for new loads. Dad had made some deal with the dozer operator, so that part was taken care of. But he also needed a couple of laborers to do some leveling with shovels. For that, Dad hired some of the countless former P.O.W.s that were constantly drifting through. They had been released from American, British, and French P.O.W. camps. We fed them, but their main desire was for American cigarettes. They would have been happy to get one cigarette per day, such were their cravings. We were able to trade for cigarettes with our American friends and whenever Dad had them, he always gave the workers extras. They loved it.

When the landfill was completed and the surface leveled, Dad traded a parcel of our land for useful tangibles. Later, as the new currency was introduced in 1948, he again took up his automotive parts and accessory business, but on a much smaller scale than before. He didn't go back to Munich, but stayed in Starnberg. He had a part of the lower level of our big house converted to a store and that was where Dad reestablished his business. Dad knew it wasn't an ideal situation and it wasn't anything like what it used to be, but we got by.

Chapter Sixteen

Dark Dealings

During the last years of the war, as rations had grown ever smaller and everything had become more scarce, there undeniably had existed a limited amount of Black Market activities throughout Germany and the rest of Europe. It all had to be handled extremely hush-hush, of course, for getting caught by the law meant severe and extreme punishment. Also, one never knew which dyed-in-the-wool Nazi might turn you in to further his own advancement in their hierarchy, or who might fink on you just out of pure jealousy.

The end of the war, however, changed this picture quite drastically. At first, there were some confined dealings starting up between some enterprising GIs and hungry German civilians that still possessed trade-able valuables. Both sides, however, had to be careful not to get caught.

After the American military had stopped the three day rampage of murdering and plundering by the re-leased inmates of Nazi concentration camps, some of these nevertheless kept right on with their criminal activities. They had been hardened criminals to start with. When U.S. authorities caught them still committing serious crimes, they were once again interned in detention camps. What became of them was unknown to us, but rumor had it that they were treated as "Displaced Persons" and shipped Stateside or to another country of their choosing.

Others banded together and formed a regular union, calling themselves V.V.N., meaning association of subjects persecuted by the Nazi-regime. This association of former inmates was soon officially recognized and forthwith started receiving food and other donations from charitable organizations worldwide.

Donations for them kept arriving in ever larger quantities. What wasn't needed was hoarded by the recipients and ended up on the "black market," which experienced a renaissance of unbelievable proportions. There, the starving German population was brutally milked of what little valuables they had left in return for small portions of coffee, chocolate, cigarettes and practically everything one could imagine.

Many times my parents had sent me to a certain house in our town where two families, members of the V.V.N., resided. I usually carried some piece of jewelry, or a camera, or some silver coins and was told to trade it for items my parents had written down just like on a grocery list. What Mr. Waxman didn't have, I received from Mr. Wandersman or vice versa. At home I had been instructed to be nice and polite to these people, but inwardly I detested having to deal with what I perceived as riff raff. While they were nice enough to me and sometimes invited me to stay awhile, I always got out of there as fast as possible without appearing rude. I was eleven years old at the time and I just did not feel safe with them. The varied goods I brought away from there, however, quickly made up for all my childish fears and anxieties. There was Cadbury chocolate from England, Maxwell House coffee and cigarettes from America, sweetened, canned condensed milk from Switzerland and many more delectable goodies too numerous to remember. These transactions still had to be handled discretely, however. While the law in those particular instances didn't care or looked the other way, the ever present danger was getting caught by a stranger with these goods on you. He could snatch your treasures from you and you could count yourself lucky not to be hit over the head, or worse, in the process.

The currency at the time was still the Reichsmark, but there was little demand for that on the "black market." While a pound of butter at the store (if it had been available) was sold for RM 1.60, the price on the Black Market was RM 800.00 for one pound of salted American butter. Most of the time, money wasn't even accepted there. It didn't help much that everyone seemed to have money. You couldn't eat it.

These V.V.N. entrepreneurs, of course, made out like bandits, but for some even that was apparently not good enough. Ever growing greed had lead some of them to quite macabre extremes. Children suddenly started mysteriously disappearing. This involved children from the age of two, who were snatched from unwatched baby carriages up to the ages of twelve who never returned home from school. Slave traders were at first suspected to be at work, but when the truth was finally discovered, it turned out to be far more grim than that. Where the only meat available at the Black Market so far had consisted just of canned products such as corned beef, suddenly fresh veal was being offered. The response was incredible. The average German hadn't had fresh veal for many years and some traded their last piece of jewelry or a golden wedding band for such a rare treat. As the demand for veal increased, so did the supply. At least for awhile.

Then one day, the newspaper headlines were full of reports about the discovery of a private, makeshift slaughterhouse in some basement. According to the papers, members of the V.V.N. had been caught red-handed, butchering two children, who had disappeared that very day from a school field trip. The meat was on its way to the "black market," to be sold to German citizens as fresh veal. When I first heard about this, it had caused an awful memory to resurface: Just how lucky had I been on that moonlit winter night last January, when I had had that close call? I felt tiny, hard goosebumps rising on my skin.

The German population and the American authorities were equally outraged. The perpetrators were arrested and held in jail to be tried by an American court. A few of those fiends were hauled out of jail one night by a mob of outraged citizens and they were swiftly lynched before American MPs could or would intervene.

While these incidents had started out as isolated cases and had never been widespread, the frequency did increase somewhat due to the increase in demand. Several other such operations were discovered, during the next few months. These discoveries, however, meant essentially the end of those deplorable undertakings. Overnight, the demand for fresh veal had ceased. Except for this one item, however, the Black Market flourished, as never before.

In 1948, the arrival of the new German currency, the Deutsche Mark, changed all this. The old Reichs Mark no longer served as currency. Practically overnight, the stores were filled with consumer goods of every description. There were foods and fruits, not seen for the last nine years, in abundant profusion. Gone were the long lines in front of the stores. Where the merchants used to complain about lack of merchandise, they were now griping about the lack of well-heeled customers. All one needed now was money.

Every German citizen had received forty Deutsche Mark. Existing bank accounts and old currencies were devaluated ten to one, but this process dragged on for years. But now, money had real value once again. A new bicycle could be bought for less than one-hundred Marks and the cost of one of the first Volkswagens was just under four-thousand Marks. The exchange rate with the United States dollar was 4.25 DM to 1 dollar.

The Black Market, however, didn't exactly die, it just shifted to other goods and priorities. Gasoline, for instance, still on rations for several years to come, was one of the most wanted commodities available in exchange for the esteemed Deutsche Mark.

The author with his parents — 1952.

Chapter Seventeen

The Interim

The years went by. I left high school at the age of fourteen and entered a four year apprenticeship at a Mercedes dealership, to learn the trade of Automotive Technician. There were no wages paid, only a little pocket money. I lived with my parents, until the apprenticeship was over. Passing the state exams with an award for excellence, I had no problems staying on with Mercedes as a journeyman technician. Now the pay was enough to support me and I enjoyed what I was doing. The German economy had recovered with leaps and bounds and the long awaited peacetime, with all its virtues and advantages had finally materialized.

Dad's automotive supply store, across the street from Starnberg's town hall — 1955.

My father had moved his business, an automotive parts and accessories store, from our home to the center of town. There he had rented a large store with seven display windows in an excellent location.

Dad's business was doing pretty well and it provided a modest living. But every so often, Dad would have problems with his war injuries. The projectile that was still lodged inside him would occasionally press against his spine, irritating a nerve. This caused him to have to stay in bed for weeks or sometimes even months. Mother would call me then to ask if I could come home and help run the business. My employers were very understanding and assured me that when my father was well again, my job would still be there waiting for me. So I frequently went home to help out and really valued the new experiences.

Unfortunately, when Dad was well enough to take over once again, we often didn't agree on business matters. I had seen the tremendous potential of his operation and had secured some lucrative orders from large firms and government agencies, but Dad did not favor the expansion. Instead of praise or maybe even a little bonus, he was critical of my initiative. At the time I could not perceive that Dad's spirit had been broken when he had come home from the war, severely wounded, only to find his entire life's accomplishments irretrievably lost. All he wanted now was to earn a modest living. I soon went back to work for Mercedes.

One October weekend of 1955, I met a girl who worked as a nurse in a nearby children's hospital. Gisela and I fell in love and after a year of dating decided to get married. Both our parents, however, vehemently opposed our intentions and tried their best to break up our engagement. Gisela's mother had the fixation to marry her daughter to some nobility. My mother, by now even more domineering than ever, insisted that I marry a girl with lots of money. Both our fathers deemed us much too young for marriage. We received no sympathy, we only had each other. But that proved to be enough. We were married by a Justice of the Peace. We couldn't afford a church wedding without the help of our parents, so that had to be postponed, for a while.

Now that we were married, our troubles were not over. Our mothers hadn't given up and tried everything in their power to break up our marriage. After a little over a year, Thomas, our first son was born, but not even that changed their attitudes. The resulting pressure on us was extremely intense. In order to save our health, our sanity and our love for each other, we decided to move as far away as possible.

From childhood on, I had always dreamed of going to America, to see where all these friendly GIs had come from, so America came to mind first. We checked with the American consulate, but found out that it was not feasible for us to immigrate to that country. We had nobody in the States that could sponsor us, no binding job offer and not enough money to satisfy the United States Immigration requirements at that time. Deeply disillusioned, we decided to emigrate to Canada.

This turned out to be a lot less complicated. We chose the part of the country where the people spoke English. I hoped I had learned enough English in high school to get by, neither one of us had the desire to learn to speak French. In January of 1958, the three of us arrived in Winnipeg, Manitoba, where I started working as a technician for the local Cadillac dealership. Canada's economy at the time, however, was anything but good. While I was able to earn a decent living during the few short summer months, the winter months turned out to be unnerving. I had no guaranteed salary, but worked strictly on commissions. The long winters brought large segments of the economy to a virtual standstill, but the bills still needed to be paid.

After a little over four years, we decided to try once more to come to the United States. We had three boys by then and another long winter was looming not far ahead. This time, it all happened relatively fast and easy. We wanted to go where there was no snow. That meant either Florida or California. The choice seemed inconsequential, since we knew little about either place and it was almost by the flip of a coin that we decided on California. I was able to secure a binding job offer from a Cadillac dealership in that state. That was enough to qualify us for immigration. We bought an old utility trailer, packed up our few belongings, and started to leave for warmer climates and hopefully better economic possibilities. Our friends and neighbors hated to see us leave.

"Who do you know in the States?" they asked.

"Nobody," we answered, "But then we didn't know anyone in Canada before we arrived here. We have each other and that will be enough."

*

California turned out to be picturesque and attractive. We thoroughly enjoyed the absence of cold weather and snow at first. I worked at the dealership in San Diego and was able to earn a decent living for us. But, while our monetary situation was better than it had been in Canada, I felt that we were really not progressing financially. Gisela suggested I start my own business in my trade, but with a wife and three children, I didn't have the courage to risk such a venture at that time. Then, friends told us about Northern Virginia and the excellent possibilities that were available there. They had lived there once and were ready to move back to what they called a stable economy. They told us that because of the close proximity to Washington, D.C. with the Federal Government, the Pentagon, and three major military bases, they had never experienced a shortage of jobs. The area, according to our friends, was virtually recession-proof.

Once again, we sold what we could of our furniture, loaded the rest on our trailer and accompanied our friends to Alexandria, Virginia. We arrived in March of 1965 and I was hired by the local Cadillac dealership. I worked there for several years. We liked Virginia and enjoyed the four distinct seasons, in spite of the occasional snowstorms. While we had relished the absence of snow in Southern California, we had also begun to miss the different seasons of the year.

Economically, things worked out perfectly for us in Virginia. We bought a house in a suburb and it wasn't long before I started my own business. I rented a suitable building and opened an autoelectric and air conditioning specialty shop. The results were phenomenal. This type of operation had practically no competition in that area. After only one year, I bought a building of my own. We prospered and soon our shop enjoyed an excellent reputation far and wide.

Chapter Eighteen

A Bittersweet Reunion

Now, as before in Canada and again in California, I often thought about my childhood friend and bene-factor, Mr. Sonn. Through telephone information, I had, over the years, tried several times to locate him, but there was no listing under his name. The only lead I had was that in the fall of 1945, he had gone back to his family in Passaic, New Jersey. It was now decades later and he could have moved many times since. There was no telling where he was at this time, or even if he was still alive. However, now we were living that much closer to where I thought him to be and so I attempted once again to find him. At first, I had the same results as before. Then one day it occurred to me that he must have family or relatives with the same last name. I asked the operator for any other listings with the last name of Sonn. She finally came up with only one, a Steve Sonn in Passaic. When I finally reached him, I soon found out that the man I was looking for was, in fact, his father. For some reason, he seemed to hesi-tate at first, but then he gave me a number where he said I could reach him.

Never will I forget that evening. When we called that number, a woman answered. As I asked to speak to Mr. John Sonn she started asking me all kinds of questions. She wanted to know who I was, how I knew of Mr. Sonn and what I wanted from him. It all seemed so strange, and I began to wonder. I had no choice, but to explain to this stranger the whole situation. At first, she didn't seem to believe a word I was saying and made no effort to get him on the phone. I had gathered by now that he really was there and insisted on talking to him personally. She finally gave in and went to get him. After a while, a timid male voice said hello. I asked him if he had been stationed in Starnberg, Germany in 1945. When he acknowledged that he had, I knew it had to be the right man. I asked him if he remembered the little boy from next door to the field kitchen.

"Of course," he said. He cited my first name and suddenly his voice sounded actually happy. He remembered.

At hearing his voice again after so many years, my eyes filled with tears and my voice eluded me for a moment. I was so overjoyed. Then I told him that I was that little boy from long ago and that I would love to see him again, as soon as possible. I asked him how we could get together. There was a long pause and when he finally did speak, his voice sounded surprisingly reserved. Little did I know at that time how embarrassed he must have felt. He apparently had no place of his own to invite me to. I had gathered by now that he had to be staying in some kind of a home or shelter. To overcome this uncomfortable dilemma, I started talking about old times and he soon warmed up again. I suggested that Gisela and I would fly to Passaic for the weekend and take him along to our hotel so we could spend some time together. He hesitated again, but there was no way that I would give up now after coming this far. I told him that we would pick him up the following weekend and to be ready. As I asked for the address, he handed the receiver back to the woman who had at first answered the phone. By now she was aware of the situation and told me how happy Mr. Sonn looked, in anticipation of our visit.

That very Saturday, a dreary January day in 1978, Gisela and I arrived in Newark, New Jersey and had a cab take us to the address we had been given. The cabby gave us a surprised look and asked if we really wanted to go there.

"Of course," I said, somewhat annoyed. "What's wrong with that?" I wanted to know. He told us that it was an especially rough neighborhood. I told him that I could handle it and away we went. The closer we came, the more I had to agree with our cabby, it really was a shabby neighborhood. But I didn't care. For Mr. Sonn I would have gone to hell and back. We finally stopped in front of a five story walk-up in bad repair. I asked the driver to wait. Gisela stayed in the cab, while I went to get Mr. Sonn. Now came the big moment when I would finally see my old friend again, after more than thirty-two years!

An elderly woman opened and when I told her who I was, she asked me in, calling back over her shoulder, "Johnny, your friend is here." We were in a long hallway. There were benches and chairs along the walls and old men sat around everywhere. One of them got up and approached us. I recognized him instantly, but still I was shocked by what I saw. I only hoped it wouldn't show on my face. I had remembered him as a tall man, strong and full of life. He had been a half a head taller than my Dad. Of course, I had been ten years old at the time and just about any grown man had appeared tall to me. But that wasn't all. He looked frail, fragile and weak. I found it hard to believe what time had done to him. I got the feeling that the years seem to extract more of a toll from the good than the bad. It took me awhile to adjust to it. It must have been similar for him; all he remembered was a little ten year old boy and now here stood this big stranger towering over him. But he seemed as happy to see me as I was to see him. John, that's how he wanted to be called now, took me back to his room to get his coat.

The room was a dark and dingy cubbyhole, with two cots and not much of anything else. On one of the cots laid an old man, constantly babbling away to himself. Once in awhile, he would let out a piercing shriek and then he would continue with his babbling.

"He's as crazy as a loon," John explained, "I can't wait to get out of here."

By now, I shared his feeling and we hurried down the hall to the front door as quickly as we could. But we were stopped by the old woman. She wanted to know how long John would be gone and I had to promise to bring him back. I also had to sign him out. We both felt relieved, as we stepped out into the grey winter day. I introduced John to Gisela and then had the cabby take us to our hotel.

When we arrived at our room, we made ourselves at home. Room service brought food and drinks and soon John and I began to reminisce about the old days in Starnberg. I still found it hard to believe that we had finally found him again. John wanted to hear all about us and our lives, but every time we tried to steer the conversation to his experiences he insisted to hear more about us first. We finally asked him to tell us about himself and mainly what he was doing in that awful place where we had found him. John took a long draught from his drink, leaned back in his chair and began his meager story. He claimed he didn't remember how he got there and didn't know why he had to stay there. He had been told that he had been found lying in the street one night, robbed and severely beaten. But that had been a long time ago, he said.

Back in Germany, John had never talked much about his life in the States or what he had been doing for a living. That was allright. In my innocent and childish way of thinking, I never could have imagined him as anything but the American soldier we had become so fond of. He had told us that he was married to a woman of Russian descent and he had showed us a picture of the two of them holding their first baby boy.

"But John," we asked, "you had a family and at least one son. Why don't they take care of you?"

For a long moment he looked through the large picture window and gazed at the New York skyline across the river. "My wife left me a long time ago," he began again, "and my five children prefer to have nothing to do with me. I have been alone for many years; nobody seems to care."

A somber expression had started to creep over his face, then he said,

"I must get after my son, Steve, to get me out of this dump, before I lose my sanity as well. Most of them in there are crazy," he continued, "and I can't imagine how he could leave me in such a place."

We asked him what kind of a place that was, but he wasn't sure, he thought it was some kind of a nuthouse.

It turned out that Steve was the only family member with whom he was even remotely in contact. I couldn't believe what I had heard, but John wouldn't say anymore. We wanted to know all about his life in these many years, but he told us very little about himself. He said that for several years he had been working in a factory that produced seat covers for the major auto-makers, but that was all he would say. We didn't push it. We figured he'll tell us what he wanted us to know, the rest didn't matter. We tried to call his son, but nobody answered the phone. I promised John that we would get in touch with Steve and see what could be done to get him away from there. That immediately brightened his spirit and he soon became his old, happy-go-lucky self again.

The author with John Sonn, two friends,
reunited after 32 years — January 29, 1978.

That evening, we took John to the nearby Sheraton, where we enjoyed a fascinating floor show. Then we relished a delicious supper together. John savored it all to the fullest. For several hours, we sat there over drinks, reminiscing and enjoying each other's company in these pleasant surroundings. Later, when we got back to our room at the Marriott, we once again sat together and, over drinks and with amiable talk, time flew by unnoticed. We had arranged for an extra room for John right next to ours and when the time came to retire, we were assured that John could sleep undisturbed and in a comfortable bed, at least for one night. The next day was also spent with pleasant conversation, good food and drink, but the evening and the hour of parting came soon enough. We dropped John off at the shelter where I had to sign him in again. We promised each other to write on a frequent basis and then a cab took us to the airport for our flight back to Virginia.

This trip had been quite an experience for us. This long awaited reunion had left a kind of a bittersweet taste. We still couldn't believe that a good man like John had to live out his old days in such obvious misery without anyone of his family really caring. We reminded ourselves that often there were two sides to a given circumstance, but we only knew his side and that was really all we cared to know. It was his well-being that mattered to us, nothing else. As soon as we got home I telephoned Steve Sonn and told him about the weekend we had spent in New Jersey and about his father's depressed condition. I tried to find out more about his father and the circumstances leading to his presence at this sorry shelter, but Steve Sonn wouldn't volunteer any information. I did, however, come away with his promise that he would find better lodgings for his father without delay. Somehow I believed him.

In the following weeks, we wrote several times to see how John was getting along, but received no answer. Then I called the shelter and was told that John's son had taken his father out of there and had moved him to a small apartment in Passaic. I got an address, but no phone number. We immediately wrote to that new address and in due time came a reply. John's letter said that he was well and happy to be out of that "loony-bin," as he called it. We wrote back and told him that we planned to have him spend next Christmas with us in our home. From his reply, we read that he was delighted.

It was a few days before Christmas. Gisela had lavishly decorated our home for the season, as she always did, and everything was ready for the holidays. I had just bought a new Ford Bronco and the first trip with it would be to New Jersey to pick up John. Arriving in his neighborhood around 9 a.m., I soon found the old tenement house where John now lived.

His place was a small efficiency on the ground floor. John was still sleeping when I knocked on his door. We both were happy to see each other again. While John got ready, I let my eyes wander, surveying his room. It was small, but the lack of furnishings made it seem more than adequate. The floor was bare, there was a bed, a table, two chairs and a wardrobe. Around the corner was a small kitchenette with a hot plate, a small refrigerator and a cabinet for groceries. It all looked like he had just moved in and wasn't quite unpacked yet, but he had been living there now for over seven months.

"It ain't much," he tried to apologize as he noticed my concerned expression, "but you can't believe how happy I am to be out of that awful loony-bin."

"You're right there," I agreed, "but how do you make out here?" I wanted to know.

"My son and his wife bring me my groceries and look after me once or sometimes twice a week," he explained, "for that I have to sign over my Social

Security check," he added with a sour grin.

Then John offered to fix breakfast for us, but I suggested we get some on the road. John packed a little suitcase that had been hidden under his bed and we turned to leave.

"Good riddance," I heard him mumble as he locked the door behind him, then he turned to me and flashed one of his happy smiles. He was ready to go.

We drove to a diner and after breakfast, we had a pleasant trip. We talked about the old days, exchanged opinions and had a grand old time. John wanted to know so much about Germany and frequently switched to the German language, which he remembered surprisingly well.

"I have always been very interested in Germany and have followed her history avidly," he began. "But there are so many things I just could not understand. For instance, if Hitler was so evil as everyone says he was, then why did he have such an immense following that brought him to power?"

"Johnny," I said, "I was too young to observe the beginnings. As a matter of fact, I wasn't even born then. I can only tell you what I have heard from other, much older people: Germany had been beaten down by the severe and humiliating impositions placed on it after the first World War. These had caused rampant unemployment and runaway inflation such as the world had never seen before. Most everyone was hungry or had hungry mouths to feed, and there was no hope. Along comes a man like Hitler, promises change, puts you to work and feeds you and your family. Now honestly, Johnny, who would *you* vote for?"

"Hitler did all that? How?" John asked.

"Through an organized public works program he called 'Arbeitsdienst'," I explained. "It was very similar to what F.D. Roosevelt did in this country. One monumental chore of the Arbeitsdienst was the construction of the 'Autobahn', a gigantic network of super freeways throughout Germany. Now there was foresight! To this day, the network of the Autobahn is still being expanded. Without it, Germany could not possibly function. So far, there was nothing bad associated with Hitler."

"Well," he conceded after some thought, "that seems to make sense. I believe I can sympathize with those hungry multitudes. But there is another factor that I could never explain: If Germany was so poor at the time, where did Hitler get the money to build up his huge and mighty Wehrmacht?"

"Hah, it's funny," I smiled, reminiscing, "I remember asking that very same question of my mother when I was a little boy."

"And what did your mother have to say," he asked me.

"She said that Hitler had to have outside help from somewhere," I answered.

"And where would that outside help have come from," he asked.

"Johnny, living as close to New York and to Wall Street as you do, you should have figured that one out long ago."

His expression became somber and for a long time John made no reply.

"You know, I had always suspected something like that," he said after a long while. "The more I think about it, the more sense it all makes. And now, from that very same quarter come the relentless efforts to never let the holocaust memory die, and to forever keep the old hate alive."

"John, the holocaust was not the only atrocity performed in that war." I replied. "Don't get me wrong, I'm not trying to minimize these actions, but there were other atrocities committed that no one hears about anymore nowadays. For instance, on April 19, 1945, a hospital train, filled with over four hundred wounded, was attacked by fifty British "Lightning" war planes. There were no survivors. Then just think of the bomb attack on Dresden, where an estimated two hundred forty-five thousand innocent civilians died in firestorms of unimaginable ferocity. This no longer had anything to do with conventional warfare. This was definitely an act of premeditated mass-murder. But no one talks about that anymore, all one still hears about is the holocaust."

"You're so right," John said, "I had never heard about Dresden."

"There you see what I mean, John. Yes, what the Nazis did at various concentration camps all over Europe had to be some of the worst war crimes, judging by numbers of victims. But then, next in line, and committed by the Allies, comes Dresden. Last, but not least, there was the senseless slaughter of two hundred ten thousand innocent Japanese civilians by the atomic bombs in Hiroshima and Nagasaki. These last two attacks were sometimes justified by claiming to force a quick end to the war, lives were actually being saved. I can't help ask if the same could not have been achieved by dropping these bombs on military targets instead of on purely residential centers.

"But, you know, I believe it is wrong to eternally dwell on these evil events. We should be looking to the here and now and to the future. Somehow I have this awful feeling that if these old hates are kept alive by constantly harping on past injustices, it might just cultivate a fertile soil through which these horrors could one day start all over again."

"A point well taken," John mused, "if more people would consider this it would help to make for a better world to coexist in, I think."

For a long while, we drove on in silence, each of us absorbed with his own thoughts. Then, finally, John spoke again.

"Another thing I could never understand, was how Germany recovered so fast and so dramatically after the war. I have seen the destruction of the cities, the transportation system, the industries and the factories, and I deemed Germany finished for a long time to come. To see Germany bounce back as fast as it did amazed me, along with many others here, to no end."

"German people as a whole are industrious, disciplined, resourceful, and hard to put down," I started to explain, "but it all would never have been possible, at least not in that short time, had it not been for the wise foresight of General Marshall and his 'Marshall-Plan'."

"I knew about that," he replied, "and I remember that he had an extremely difficult time with our Congress. So many senators and congressmen, for reasons of their own, had vehemently opposed him and his proposal, and had fought him every step of the way. I guess they would have preferred to see the 'Morgenthau-Plan' adopted."

"Johnny," I said, "I have lived in the United States for quite awhile now and I have seen Congress successfully defeat a number of great proposals in the past."

"I know what you mean," he interrupted, "Just think back to 1945 when, after Germany's surrender, General Patton wanted to consolidate with what was left of the German Wehrmacht to march against and defeat the Soviet Union. There would have never been a Cold War with its tremendous arms race. Congress knew it, but again for reasons of their own, would not allow it."

"The concept of the American government seems a fine thing," I pondered, "but if too many of the wrong people get into Congress it seems it becomes quite counterproductive, at times. As taxpayers, of course, we have to pick up the tab."

"Yeah, and what irks me the most," he clamored, "is how they can stay on for ever and ever. The millions and millions they spend to get re-elected shows me that a lot of them are in there not to serve the people, but to stuff their own pockets with money from special interest groups and lobbies. I can't imagine anyone spending that kind of money, without expecting it all back and a healthy profit to boot."

He seemed quite upset by now, so I quickly said, "Johnny, I think we're getting too deep into politics, we can't change it, let's try and talk about more cheerful topics."

"You're right," he was smiling again, "No sense in our trying to fix the world. But how were the years after the war in Germany?" John wanted to know.

"What comes to my mind immediately, is how we, as children, had had fun playing cops and robbers with real live guns and ammunition. I know I told you about that before you left Germany and was surprised how horrified you had been to learn about this. At the time, it had been a tremendous excitement for us kids, we finally had toys! To think back and relive all we had done then, gives me the shivers now. But, I know that doesn't answer your question, John."

"Yes," he nodded, "to hear about your playthings was unthinkable for me then and even now. I remember making you promise never to do that anymore. Tell me," he said, "did you keep your promise?"

"Well, Daddy was home by then and he kept me pretty busy. There wasn't much time left for me to sneak off into the woods. Let's just say, I survived it," I grinned.

"John, I remember how heartbroken you had been when you had seen firsthand the devastation of Munich. I think this might interest you. Years later, the details of the air-raids on Munich that had started as early as June 5, 1940 became known. Altogether, there had been 74 major air-raids on Munich.

This panorama of Munich greeted the first
U.S. invasion troops — May 1, 1945.

A tally of bombs dropped on the city totaled:

450 of the highly devastating air-mines (block-busters,) 61,000 T.N.T. explosive bombs, 145,000 liquid fire-bombs, 3,316,000 stick bombs (bombs containing highly flammable phosphorus.)

Result: In the city of Munich, with a population of about one million people, 81,500 homes were destroyed, leaving 300,000 civilians either homeless severely wounded or dead.

"But, let's get back to your question about Germany after the war. For about three years," I began, "things were basically the same for us as they were when you were there. Then came the new currency and with it the long awaited peacetime that everyone had been longing for. There were a number of great years. Everybody was busy rebuilding. The German economy grew with leaps and bounds and there was no unemployment. Even the money lenders gradually returned. They weren't acting quite as blatantly, as before. Their methods were more sophisticated now (now there were credit cards,) but nevertheless, they were back. All in all, everybody was happy and content. The population enjoyed and appreciated what they had. They remembered how rough it had been and were thankful. Now it's different. It seems just about everybody tries to live high on the hog, as they say here, and they take it all for granted. The younger generations have no idea of the suffering that the war had brought. For them it all seems as obscure as peacetime had seemed to us at the time. But now, John, why don't you tell me about yourself and how things went with you?" I asked.

Again, I wanted to know so much more about him and his life, since he had left Germany, but his answers were vague and slow in coming. He had apparently worked at factory jobs most of his life. He told me that, at one point, his wife had left him and had taken their children with her. He said he had no contact with any of them and that, of course, he missed them. It was largely what he had already told us awhile back at the hotel in New Jersey. That was all he would say and I didn't push it.

After about a six-hour ride, we arrived in Virginia, hungry and tired. When John saw the lovely Christmas decorations that Gisela had put up throughout our home, he seemed truly moved.

We sat together till late that night, talking about old times, enjoying food, drink and the comforts of our home. John was a heavy smoker. We normally didn't allow smoking in our home, but with John we just *had* to make an exception. Only the youngest of our four children, our daughter, Irene, was still living at home. We had adopted Irene in Alexandria, Virginia, when she was two months old. By now she was in middle school. John and Irene got along famously. We had decided to spend Christmas at our lakehouse about sixty miles to the south. So the next morning we packed up the car and drove to our weekend retreat. When we arrived there, the lake lay still, largely frozen over and peaceful. The surrounding hills presented a beautiful frame to a picture of serene loveliness. The snow on the fields was unmarred by any tracks and the dark evergreen's branches hung low under their burden of snow. The air was crisp and clear and it all seemed like a picture on a Christmas card.

The house was soon aired out and heated. We all helped with unpacking the car. Our Christmas tree had been set up at our home, so Gisela sent John and me to cut a live tree for us here. I remember looking high and low for a good, evenly grown tree. The pretty ones, however, were too large and none of the smaller ones were even. We decided on the best-looking of the small trees, cut it and brought it in to be decorated. Gisela was very disappointed.

"What kind of *tree* did you guys bring me?" she complained. "This thing looks like a broom."

"It'll look better once you've put the decorations up," we told her, but she wasn't convinced. After it was decorated, I had to admit that it really didn't look like much, but it nevertheless created some atmosphere and that's what counted.

When the time came, we exchanged presents and settled in to celebrate the holidays. John really loved being with us. We spent a whole week out there in the quiet solitude of the countryside. The weather had warmed up quite a bit and only small parts of the lake were still frozen. During daytime, I took John hunting and fishing. We were rewarded with a couple of rabbits and some fine catfish. Gisela prepared them and we enjoyed her superb cooking immensely. When evening came, we talked, played games and partied, until late each night.

John Sonn reminiscing with the author
— December 1978.

Then one morning, as John came to breakfast, I noticed that something was wrong with him. I had to look again to spot it, but the white of his eyes had changed to a sickly yellow. I asked him what that was and wanted to know how he felt. He said he felt fine and claimed he didn't know anything about his eyes. I then suspected that perhaps something was wrong with his liver. I asked if any of the food or drink had disagreed with him, but he denied it. Gisela and I discussed it. Perhaps, John had had a drinking problem all along. We didn't know, but we were worried. We decided to no longer serve any alcohol and drank coffee, coke and soda pops instead. I hated to do this to him, because I suspected that he had enjoyed his drinks. John never said anything about it. After a couple of days, we had a change of heart. After Gisela and I again discussed it, we figured that there was no sense in depriving John of something he had obviously enjoyed. He was old enough, we figured, to know what was or wasn't good for him. While we hadn't done any excessive drinking, we kept it even more in moderation. John now seemed much happier.

John really liked our home and also the lakehouse and commented on it quite often. We proudly told him we enjoyed them as well. I explained that since I had been working for myself in my own business, we could finally afford luxuries that we had only dreamed of while working for someone else. He readily agreed to that piece of insight.

One warm and sunny afternoon, we were sitting on the pier next to our boathouse, dangling pieces of wieners into the lake. Fishing had been slow, but we enjoyed the peaceful scenery, the warm rays of the winter sun, and each other's company. We started chatting about old times and one thing led to another. Pretty soon we were talking about the war again.

Suddenly John said, "What I also often wondered about was why the Jews stayed on in Germany. I remember being at an employee's party of the factory I worked for. At some point the conversation had turned to the Jews living in Germany, during the uneasy four or five years before the Wehrmacht rolled into Poland and the festivities began in earnest. I remember telling a Jewish stockholder who had lost his grandfather in a concentration camp that I didn't understand why the Jews in Germany, or all over Europe, but especially in Germany, hadn't gotten out while there was still time. They were not, by and large, stupid people, and many had had firsthand experience of such persecution. Surely they had seen what was coming. So why had they stayed? He didn't say it directly, but I got the message. If you have a good thing going for you, you find it hard to give it up. One of these good things he referred to had become instantly obvious to me — money lending."

"Again, Johnny, that was before my time. I can only tell you about the general consensus of the population and what is documented in historic reports. I can tell you this — Hitler told the Jews in Germany, in 1937, to get out and gave them three months to do so. He allowed them to take their precious paintings, their grand pianos, their gold and silver, their hoards with them. A great many did just that and they were welcomed with open arms in New York. Most of them, however, did not heed the warning and stayed. After three months, Hitler told them again to get out. This time they were not allowed to take their hoards out with them. Again, many left, and here we come to a very little known fact — when their ships reached New York, they were not allowed to disembark. In full view of the statue of liberty, their own brethren ordered the ships turned around to take these people back to Germany. They were not wanted here, they had brought no money. Thirty four other nations refused to grant asylum to any Jewish refugees as well."

"I'd heard about this a long time ago," John interceded, "but not many here believe that this could have happened."

"Yes, they sent them back, knowing good and well what might happen to them. Many Jews, however, refused to leave Germany. Some thought that Hitler and his Nazi regime probably wouldn't last very long, so why should they leave a good thing behind. But then the persecution started in earnest. On November 9, 1938, Ernst von Rath, the German Attache in Paris, was assassinated by Herschel Grünspan, a Polish Jew. In retaliation for that assassination, the Nazis started to break the windows of some Jewish stores and destroyed their merchandise. Because of all the broken glass it became known as the "Reichskristallnacht." From then on, Jews had to wear a yellow star on their outer garments that clearly identified them as Jews and the German public was forbidden to associate or do business with them. A number of the more belligerent Jews were rounded up and put into concentration camps.

"Now I really wished that they would have left while they still could. When the details of the 'Morgenthau Plan' had leaked out in September 1944, the German population was outraged. Now, our propaganda minister Dr. Josef Göbbels had no problem manipulating the general sentiment against all Jews. He exploited this new revelation to the fullest, calling for renewed efforts to cleanse at least Germany's economy of any Jewish domination. The threat of what 'the International Jewish Clique', as he called it, had in store for us, should we lose the war, rekindled every German's determination to win this war. It seemed to have brought it all to a point. From then on, fewer and fewer Jews were seen on the streets, their fate had become a lot more severe. I suppose the exterminations, we heard about so much later, had now begun."

"Tell me," John asked, "did the German people know what happened to them and did they know about these extermination camps?"

"Absolutely not. We had no idea. I remember the general outrage of the people, when the Allies published the first photographs of what they had found in some of the concentration camps. We absolutely refused to believe that this was for real. For a long time, we suspected that the Allies had faked these pictures and reports for reasons of their own. When it finally became clear that some of these reports were true after all, the public still found it hard to believe. That Jews as a whole, were not altogether well liked in Germany was no secret. That, with the revelation of the infamous 'Morgenthau Plan', a lot of them disappeared into concentration camps was also pretty common knowledge. However, details of what happened to some of them were not known by the German population."

"Might you be saying this to justify these deeds?" John asked. I couldn't believe he was saying that. I felt highly irritated.

"John," I said, trying to stay calm, "I don't have to justify anything to anybody. I was ten years old when the war was over, remember? I could not have hurt anybody and what some Nazis did behind the scenes was certainly not within my control."

"Sorry, it was just a silly thought."

"It's all right, Johnny. What you probably didn't know was that we Germans had been every bit as afraid of ending up in one of these camps as the Jews were.

To give you an example: In 1933, when the Nazis came to power, they started doing away with any form of labor unions. All other political parties were outlawed by then. Before that, my grandfather had sat at the board of directors of one of the largest construction firms in Munich. He had been representing a union and had also been a member of the Christian Democratic Party. All things that the Nazis detested. As Nazis infiltrated the leadership of the firm, they threw my grandfather out. Grandpa never did have any use for the Nazis and he had always been very outspoken. He let them know what he thought of them and would have surely ended up in a concentration camp. My father had seen what was coming and quickly intervened. He convinced Grandpa to come and act as general manager in Dad's business. So you see, Johnny, no one was really safe in those days."

"Well, one hears so much," John reflected, "and most of it is just hearsay. It's good to hear from someone who was really there, has lived through it and can tell you firsthand how it really was."

"Yes, there are lots of rumors of all kind," I said. "There are even people who insist that Hitler did not personally know of the exterminations, that it all was done by his Nazi henchmen. These people go to great length to research Nazi documents and make their case on the fact that not a single such order or paper has ever been found that bore Hitler's signature. They admit that Hitler had no use for the Jews and had wanted them out of the country and later on out of Europe. Hitler had called this the 'final solution'. But they say he knew nothing of a death camp. I, for one find that hard to believe. If Hitler really never gave that order, he certainly would have found out about it sooner or later. By then, he probably didn't care. The end justified his means."

Suddenly John's fishing rod fell from his hands and started sliding along the pier. Just before it went over the edge, I was able to put my foot on it and stop it. I picked it up, felt the tug of a heavy fish and set the hook. Handing his rod back, I told him, "Good luck, Johnny, it feels like a good one." He got up and fought the fish bravely. When it rolled near the surface, we could see that it really was a big fish. I suggested he'd walk over to the shoreline, as to not get it tangled in the pilings of the pier. Meanwhile, I got the landing net from the boathouse. The fish had not yet given up, but John had moved it a good ways down the shoreline and out of harms way. When it was finally played out, I netted it for him. It was a superb channel catfish and it weighed just over eighteen pounds. I could see the pride in John's eyes as he walked up to the house to show off his prize.

We fished and hunted together a couple more days, but time flew by much too fast. We had to get back to the city eventually.

Back at home, when John saw our nice and perfect Christmas tree again, he grinned,

"It really was a broom what we had out there at the lake."

"Go ahead and rub it in," I joked, "not everything can be perfect."

For New Years Eve, we were invited to a party by some dear friends of ours. It turned out to be a really nice affair and John enjoyed himself tremendously. Our friends were aware of the circumstances that had brought John and us together and really took a liking to him.

Then, at one point John took our hostess aside and whispered, "You know, life can be a funny thing. You do something nice for somebody and thirty-three years later you unexpectedly get rewarded for it in such a wonderful manner. The Good Lord really works in miraculous ways."

During the course of the evening, we heard John repeat this statement several times to other guests. We were glad to see him so happy.

Then came the day where John felt he had to get back home. On our last evening together, we called my mother in Germany. We told her who was with us and how we had found John. They talked together for a while. To me, however, Mother's reaction seemed a little disappointing. John had apparently meant a lot more to me than he had ever meant to her. Children seem to be so much more impressionable.

Thinking back to my childhood, I remembered what had so much endeared the GIs, and Mr. Sonn especially, to me: I had been absolutely amazed at the friendly and tolerant nature of most of these Americans, compared to the constantly bickering, and so often ill tempered, war-stressed German civilian population. However, I long since realized that people's behavior everywhere would change under pressure and that Americans were no exception.

My thoughts flashed back to an incident in 1973. It had happened during the gasoline shortage here in the States. There had been a long line of automobiles at our neighborhood service station. The line was several blocks long and extended around a corner into another street. I had seen a motorist drive up to what he thought was the end of the line. He had been unaware that the line continued around the corner.

Suddenly dozens of horns were angrily honking and enraged people came out of their cars and started arguing with that hapless driver. A regular fist fight ensued in the middle of the street. That's when I realized that there really was no difference between the German people after the war and the American soldiers. The people were the same, but people's behavior seemed to respond to the circumstances they were subjected to. People react to pressure no matter who or where they are.

The following morning John insisted that I should not drive him back in my car, because it would be a twelve hour round trip. He said he lived around the corner from a Greyhound bus stop and suggested that I put him on the bus instead. I didn't like the idea at all, but he insisted and wouldn't have it any other way. So I got him a ticket, bought him a bottle of his favorite liquid and a couple of cartons Pall Malls. Knowing John's aversion to writing I had given him a pre-addressed post card so he could let us know that he got home all right. I told him that we would pick him up again so he could spend next Christmas with us as well. John really looked forward to that. I took him to the bus and we waved, until the heavy vehicle disappeared in the distance. Again I compared in my mind how sad I had been, when, as a child, I had seen him disappear on that army truck and had thought it would be forever. This time was different. We were both looking forward to next Christmas.

About a week later, his postcard arrived. He had made it home without incident and he thanked us again for everything. We wrote to him twice that summer but there was no answer. Then one day, his son, Steve, called and informed us that his father, my friend and benefactor, had passed away. They had found him lying on the floor of his little cubbyhole, dead. Since they did not look in on him on a daily basis, they were not certain just how long he had been dead, when they found him. I was stunned. Now I had lost him for the second time, and this time for good. All the grief of our first parting revived itself in my mind, adding to the new anguish that this phone call had brought. After the first shock, however, I felt in a way almost relieved, knowing that his misery had finally ended. I hoped and prayed that he would be better off where he was now.

There had been another American soldier who had befriended us and whom I would have liked to see again. There was, however, never any correspondence with him. All we knew was that his name was John Hendricks and that his parents had a dairy farm in Wisconsin. We found out later that Wisconsin was famous for its many dairy farms and with a common name like that, it would be next to impossible to locate the right man without even knowing the name of the town that he lived in. For most Germans of that time the enormous dimensions of the United States, or even the size of an individual State, was almost impossible to comprehend.

Epilogue

Thinking back to that very urgent question that a little boy had once asked of his mother so long ago, I can now say that I understand the meaning of peace. Better yet, I have found myself at peace with my family, my surroundings and the fine people I am in contact with.

When I retired from my business in 1990, my wife and I moved to Tyler, Texas to escape the hustle and bustle, traffic, high taxes and the stress of living in Northern Virginia. We both have found our peace here and are enjoying the laid-back life and the friendly people of Texas.

Lately, I took part in some very stimulating discussions with people from all walks of life about my childhood experiences as they appear in this manuscript. One of the most frequent questions asked were if the Allied bombers really searched out schools and hospitals as favorite targets. American civilians seem to be under the impression that such deeds simply were not done by the civilized Allies. But it was all too true. While American bombing missions concentrated mostly on destroying strategically important targets, it was the British Royal Air Force that specialized in area saturation bombing of densely populated urban residential sectors. In the summer of 1944, even Winston Churchill expressed reservation towards this type of warfare. Regardless of this, Britain's Air-marshall Arthur Travers Harris (nick-named Bomber-Harris) ordered his soldiers to continue these massacres of helpless German civilians right to the very end of the war, including the destruction of schools and hospitals. Perhaps, in some instances, it may have also been the choice of certain bomber pilots. The German population regarded it as being part of the war. They knew that this was done to invoke terror and chaos on the civilian population. They also knew that through this, the enemy expected to cause despair and anarchy which, hopefully, would lead to open rebellion against the regime.

However, as it turned out, it mostly had the exact opposite effect. The German population, at least for a while, worked just so much harder to do their share to bring about a victorious ending of that horrible conflict. In the end, however, the enemy's strategies did have their desired effect. When the call for the Volkssturm came, nobody listened.

Of course, these things would not be made public to the American Nation. Our Nazis did not advertise their war crimes either and when the German Luftwaffe indiscriminately shot their V-1 and V-2 rockets across the channel, nobody could really predict where they landed and what damage they might do. Whoever wins a war can effectively ignore these despicable deeds while the crimes of the loser will be forever kept alive in the memory of all the world.

Since the completion of my manuscript, I have been invited by history classes of various schools to talk about my experiences. During these very enjoyable and interesting discussions, I repeatedly encountered the misconception that being a German soldier of that era was automatically synonymous with being a Nazi. Nothing could be further from the truth. To explain the situation, I used the following example: Lets say

one of our major political parties, for instance the Demo-
crats (but it could be either one) would achieve total
power, become involved in a war, and draft you into
the military. You, however, had always been a Republican. Would that now make you a Democrat? Most
certainly not! You would be an American Soldier, forced
to fight for a regime you don't believe in, but you would
certainly not be a Democrat. You would still, at heart,
be a Republican even if you could no longer openly pro-
fess to it.

Of course there were Nazis in every level of the
German military service, especially within Hitler's elite
fighting units, the S.S. Some of them were such fanat-
ics that they were deemed dangerous even by their fellow soldiers. But thanks to God, they were a minority.

As a closing thought about peace, I suppose that,
and this is truly sad, we cannot expect a worldwide
peace as long as there are those who instigate wars
and those who profit by them. All too often, they are
one and the same. But to me now, these things are far
removed and no longer involve me personally. The sight
and sound of aircraft have lost their terror to the point
that I immensely enjoy flying the seaplane that I own.
It is, of course, much smaller than a B-17 Flying For-
tress, but it allows me to view the world from atop,
whenever I feel the urge. I can now say, as I did on my
last visit with my mother, shortly before she passed
away,

"Mom, I now understand the meaning of *peace!*"